Homo Zappiens

Growing up in a digital age

Wim Veen
and **Ben Vrakking**

Published by Network Continuum Education
The Tower Building
11 York Road
London
SE1 7NX

www.networkcontinuum.co.uk
www.continuumbooks.com

An imprint of The Continuum International Publishing Group Ltd

First published 2006

LB 1628.3
V39 5
2006

0 7691029 0

ISBN-13: 978 1 85539 220 5
ISBN-10:   1 85539 220 8

Managing editor: Sarah Nunn
Layout by: Neil Hawkins, ndesign
Cover design by: Marc Maynard

Printed in Great Britain by MPG Books Ltd, Bodmin, Cornwall

Contents

Author's acknowledgements   5

Preface   7

Chapter 1: A time of change   15

Chapter 2: Meeting *Homo zappiens*   27

Chapter 3: Making sense of chaos   53

Chapter 4: Learning playfully   79

Chapter 5: Stopping the roller coaster   99

Chapter 6: What schools could do   111

Glossary   141

Bibilography   149

Acknowledgements   156

Index   158

Author's acknowledgements

Education systems have been evaluated, reconsidered, changed and reviewed extensively over the last decades. Many educationalists, sociologists, engineers, economists and others have been involved in discussions on how our education systems should look like in the near future. Curricula have been adapted, new learning paradigms have been launched. And in the middle of this jumble of discussions, initiatives and experiments, a new generation has grown up, a generation that did not protest, that did not start revolutionary manifestations in big cities as in the 1960s. Silently, this generation has adopted technology and has developed new strategies for living and for learning. And those strategies differ so much from former generations that a complete new actor is marching into the arena of educational change.

When I first put forward the phenomenon of *Homo zappiens* as a major change factor, it was already quite well on its way to enter nursery and primary schools. But it took some time before we realized the full consequences of this new generation for learning and our education systems as a whole. *Homo zappiens* is not only a generation doing things differently from previous generations, *Homo zappiens* is an exponent of societal changes related to globalization, individualization and the increasing uses of technology in our lives. In that sense, I consider *Homo zappiens'* values and behaviour as an opportunity to help us in reshaping education's future. Instead of considering them as a threat and neglecting their current practices, I suggest we look to this generation as a source for inspiration and guidance on how to adjust our education systems to better meet the needs of our future society.

I am very happy to write the above sentences after many friends and colleagues have encouraged me to write this book. Michelle Selinger (UK), Christina Aderklou (Sweden), Rita Minelli (Italy) and Stellan Ranebo (Sweden), they all have actively supported me in the idea that a book on this issue would be worthwhile. Colleagues in my faculty have also been chasing me to put my thoughts on paper. In particular, Peter van der Zanden often reminded me to do the things that are important instead of simply the things that must be done today. I have learned many things from my students over the years and those who have been particularly supportive in getting this book to the market were Willem van Valkenburg and Jan-Paul van Staalduinen. Many MSN conversations with them started with: 'How is the book going?' And finally there was Ben Vrakking, another outstanding student who became the co-author of the book as he liked to write down our multiple conversations on this issue. The student who taught me most, however, was my youngest son, Armand, who shared with me a logic that I also found in other studies of *Homo zappiens*. Jim Houghton, who had an excellent and positive style of getting an author to deliver a manuscript, even when it was a year later than planned! And Sarah Nunn, a great editor who helped to get the book to the printer. Thank you all for your effort and support!

Preface

❝ *They say that time changes things, but you actually have to change them yourself.* **❞**

Andy Warhol

Welcome reader! You may have started reading this book for several possible reasons; it may have been recommended to you, you may have found the authors interesting or maybe a slight bit of force was used and you were told to read this book for a reason you may never wish to know. If one of the above is the case, we sincerely hope to inspire you to become interested in the contents of our story, for that is where the other four possible reasons lie. You may have searched for a book on learning, education, technology or maybe you were interested in humans and simply misspelled 'sapiens' :-)[1] Whatever the reason, we promise you an interesting read and sufficient food for thought if you only let your mind absorb the breadth of implications and applications of the words contained within. Let us first satisfy your need for guidance. In this preface we will provide you with a brief overview of what this book contains. First, however, we will tell you what (not) to expect from this book.

---

[1] That strange symbol, only recently added to our official punctuation, is known as a smiley, for if you tilt your head to the left, you will see two eyes, a nose and a smile. If you find any words or symbols in this book that are alien to you, you may want to refer to the glossary.

Why write a book?

In times long ago, people used to gather around fires as dusk fell to listen and enact tribal lore and, thus, share experiences and preserve knowledge. Travelling poets performed their arts and stories in amphitheatres for large gatherings of people. Even today when movies can be downloaded direct to the home and frequently before they appear in cinemas outside the USA, people still go to the movies. Apparently there is more to stories than simply transferring a bit of information and performance skills.

This book was written for a specific audience. If you enjoy reading in the quiet of your own surroundings, if you like to take the time alone to reflect on your reading or if you want the full and uninterpreted version of our telling (or a part of it), you have reached for the right medium. This book is a snapshot in time of what we want to tell you.

If, however, you have picked this book up because you need the information it contains, or feel that it is the only way to perceive what is said within, then we will have to point you to other possibilities. One of the reasons for writing this book is that we feel the time for changing standards is again upon us and this, in turn, creates potential. With the aid of technology, communication is no longer restricted to text. Images and sound may be added just as easily and, apparently, add just as much, or even more, to the experience. While writing about change and the potential for more diverse and tailored education, it would be a missed opportunity not to demonstrate by example.

We are currently setting up a website **www.homozappiens.nl** where we will attempt to provide you with a campfire experience: a sharing of this story in the company of a community of interested people. We will try to give you a more illustrated version of this story online and by offering a forum for discussion and links to additional information, we wish to create a community where every member can, through the richness of interactions, discover and share what this story can add to his or her (working) life. If you are looking for an alternative to this book, please visit the site and you may find a richer, more diverse path to where you want to go. Alternatively, you may read this book, and then comment on what you found interesting or missing. It is our intention to provide readers of this book with the possibility to acquire hands-on experience on the subjects discussed herein. In a way, this website is our solution to keeping our story alive and organic.

Why should you read this book?

This book describes a view on the generation of children born with a computer mouse in their hand. It describes children who have come to discover the world through a multitude of television channels, computer games, iPods, websites, blogs and mobile phones, and it explores the implications of their behaviour for learning. In a sense, this book offers a view on how society as a whole is changing the way it learns and is by no means meant to exclude older generations from the potential of new education. We are telling you a story, the story of the 'Homo zappiens', to show you the potential for change, if we allow ourselves to reconsider practices we consider proven.

This book holds a positive view on what a new generation of learners can bring to our schools, and how teachers could respond to these students who have grown up with technology from an early age. It reflects on how things are and have been, while sketching what could be. It also gives suggestions on how to adapt our teaching practices in a society where dealing with knowledge is a matter of negotiation and creativity and where learning is a lifelong activity. It is an exciting voyage for teachers to participate in these changes that go beyond adaptations of traditional practices and in which the role of new technologies will be prominent. However, not all established customs are bad and while we describe a utopian future for learning and paint a road that may lead there, we have taken thousands of years to arrive where we are and should recognize how little really changes when we give education a new face.

Anyone interested in learning and education, be it for professional or personal reasons, as well as readers interested in the influences of technology on society, should find this book a good read. Depending on your interests, expertise and involvement with technological advances of the digital age, much in this book may trigger recognition or confirm what you have known for some time. In either case, this story may help you make sense of or find solutions to the world around you. Please remember, you may find it beneficial to visit our dedicated website (www.homozappiens.nl), especially if this book raises more questions than it answers.

Teachers and all those working in education will find three main related issues in this book:

What are *Homo zappiens* and how do they behave?

A new generation who has learned to deal with new technologies is currently coming into our educational system. This generation that we describe as *Homo zappiens* is the generation that has grown up using multiple technological devices from early childhood: the television remote control, the computer mouse, the minidisc and, more recently, the mobile phone, the iPod and the MP3 player. These devices have enabled today's children to keep control of information flows, to deal with discontinuous information and information overload, to intertwine face-to-face and virtual communities, and to communicate and collaborate in networks according to their needs.

Homo zappiens are active processors of information, skilled problem solvers using gaming strategies and effective communicators. Their relationship with school has changed fundamentally as these children consider schools as just one of the focal points in their lives. Far more important are their networking with friends, their part-time jobs and going out during weekends. *Homo zappiens* seem to consider schools as disconnected institutions, more or less irrelevant to them as far as their daily life is concerned. Inside schools they show hyperactive behaviour and short attention spans, and both teachers and parents have concerns. But *Homo zappiens* want to be in control of what they engage with and do not possess the patience to listen to a teacher explaining the world as it is according to him/her. In fact, *Homo zappiens* are digital, and school is analogue.

Do *Homo zappiens'* playful activities relate to learning?

Homo zappiens learn by playing, exploratory play. Their learning starts as soon as they play simple computer games and learning soon becomes a collective activity as problems will be solved collaboratively and creatively, acting in a global community of interest. Computer games are challenging *Homo zappiens* to find appropriate strategies to solve problems, to define and categorize problems, and a variety of other metacognitive learning skills.

In traditional education, learning was strongly related to disciplinary content. Content taught stemmed from academic disciplines and was considered as objectifiable knowledge that could be transferred to students.

Nowadays, we consider knowledge as negotiated and in an ever changing context within a specific domain. From a psychological point of view, we currently believe that learning is the mental process of individuals trying to construct knowledge from information, giving meaning to it. It is not the mere data that give us understanding of processes or phenomena; it is the interpretation of the data and information that leads to knowledge. What meaning we attribute to information is often communicated and negotiated within our community or society. We may come to the conclusion that children of today's generation do possess learning skills and strategies that are crucial for giving meaning to information and these skills and strategies are vital to future learning in a knowledge intensive economy. We may question if these skills are sufficiently recognized or valued by schools. The problem is that schools still try to transfer knowledge the way it was designed 100 years ago. This would not be a problem if every economic structure in our societies were still the same. Unfortunately, this is not the case.

What could schools do?

Recognizing the learning skills and strategies that *Homo zappiens* are developing mainly outside of school, educational institutions could respond according to the needs of these new clients. Revolutionary responses appear in countries such as the Netherlands where a small but growing number of parents no longer consider traditional schools an appropriate fit for their children and have established about 60 private schools. In addition, several school boards have also responded to the need for new learning methods by creating experimental schools where major changes have been introduced in the organization, teaching methods and approaches to content.

All of these new initiatives show five major similarities:

- Students work in time slots of four hours instead of 50 minutes.
- Students work in groups of 90 to 150 but act within basic groups of 12.
- Learning is research based, authentic and has relevance to children.
- Content is communicated through interdisciplinary themes.
- Network technology has an important role in the learning process.

Many of us may already have had experiences with *Homo zappiens* and some of us think teaching has become tougher because of them. We agree that teaching has become more challenging, that students have changed considerably in their learning and social behaviour over the last decades. We also think that there is a kind of rupture with the introduction of *Homo zappiens* in schools, a break with tradition that may present both serious threats to the educational system as it is, and challenges as teaching evolves into something more exciting; this new generation is offering unseen opportunities for making teaching a passionate and motivating profession that makes a difference to future society.

These opportunities relate to new roles, new content, and new teaching and learning methods. Teachers becoming coaches supplying expert support to children who are learning more independently on real-life issues and problems. Future society demands that its citizens be able to cope with complexity both in their private and working lives. Social networks of individuals have grown and have become more complex than before, and so have economic networks that have evolved at a global scale resulting in multinational or global economies.

As these socio-economic developments will continue, future society needs people who can address complex and fuzzy problems from different angles and come up with unexpected solutions. Acquiring content as the main goal of education will be less important, replaced instead by meaning and relevance. As a consequence, schools will no longer be institutions training children for certainty; instead they will facilitate learning for a generation that can live and work in knowledge intensive organizations and institutions where they will have to rely on skills of flexibility and adaptability to cope with ever changing conditions and situations. These economic and societal developments imply changes not only in our educational system, but more importantly in our professional beliefs, attitudes and skills. We are convinced that the effort of meeting the needs of the new generation of learners is worthwhile and that the results will be recompensing for teachers and students alike.

Some might draw a long list of arguments showing that educational changes are almost impossible to implement at any ordinary school, notably as indicated in the above mentioned bullet points (see opposite). Legislation, budget restrictions, building requirements and human factors are major obstacles and hard to bypass or surmount. The National Curriculum inhibits major changes as far as the content is concerned, school buildings are not suited for student groups of around 90, and teachers may have to be retrained extensively in order to change their teaching practice and their roles.

We might say that such changes are only possible for a minority of wealthy schools. We might also think that it is not worth it, since exam results have been sufficiently good over the last decades; so why change? And we might say that parents would not be pleased by such changes. They want their children to acquire the best certificates they know of and are reluctant to accept new diplomas which they can not yet properly value. Good points! Nobody should change anything in a system that works well. This book is not a plea for educational change as such. This book seeks to look into the world of children growing up digitally and wants to make clear what this means for learning, for schools and for teachers. For those already looking for new approaches to education, this book may well inspire you.

We will discuss the characteristics of the *Homo zappiens* and will explore the consequences of its accompanying cyber culture for learning and schools. We think this generation of *Homo zappiens* offers a chance for educational change, and a basic support for an evolving teaching profession. This book aims to understand children's behaviour, relate their behaviour to learning, and show the opportunities for teachers and schools to take advantage of children's skills, attitudes and beliefs in their effort to support students to prepare for future life, citizenship and work.

Chapter 1

A time of change

> *In times of change, learners inherit the Earth, while the learned find themselves beautifully equipped to deal with a world that no longer exists.*
>
> Eric Hoffer

A few years ago we were spooked by the media, when, with the ending of a century, we were suddenly faced with what came to be known as the 'millennium bug': embedded computer chips in a great variety of devices had been programmed to contain a six-digit date and with the passing of 1999 to 2000 there was a risk that these chips would start telling us that we were again living in the year 1900 instead of the year 2000. There was the fear that our lives and the society that we had so carefully constructed with governments, records of transactions, electronics and the like would be severely disturbed. And to add to the problem, many of the programmers of the early chips, which had been programmed in languages called FORTRAN and COBOL, had since retired taking their knowledge with them. We appeared to be headed for disaster.

We all know now that the passing of the year 1999 was uneventful in the sense that no bug came to send us back to the Stone Age. However, the example illustrates that we have become so used to technology that we can no longer imagine what we would do without it.

In this chapter, we will discuss a few of the trends in technology and society that are visible today. Also, as the story we tell in the next four chapters will stimulate you to think of how we may change the way we see and do things for the better, we think it's perhaps useful to reflect on earlier times when we faced similar transitions. This chapter may seem to be the entire history of mankind condensed into a few millimetres of pages, but we hope to offer you as many leads for reflection as we can get the publisher to publish. It is our intention to offer you a second opinion on the world around you, so that you may look at it anew and see where the story of the *Homo zappiens* fits in.

We will try gradually to take you through a day in the life of an average human male. We shall call him Jack. Jack works in the sales and marketing department of a large multinational corporation. He is responsible for canned goods. Late last night, before dozing off, Jack set his alarm by the light of a bedside lamp and read the last two pages of his book before going to sleep. It's now 7.30am and the alarm has switched on to his favourite radio station, and is playing a merry tune by Frank Sinatra. Jack is in a pensive mood today and as he walks the 20 steps from the side of his bed to the bathroom sink, he starts scratching his beard. *'What if,'* he thinks, *'what if I was living 3,000 years ago? How much of the world I know now would I really miss?'*

The first thing that comes to mind is the radio playing in the background. In ancient days there would not have been a radio; there would not have been electricity to power the radio or transmitters to transmit radio waves. There would not be the profession of disc jockey or the concept of a music label providing society with commercial music. Maybe, back then, there would not even be specialized musicians. Probably there would have been music. Jack starts humming. He just thought of how his job could have been. Instead of rushing off to work at 7.55am to beat the local traffic jam, Jack might have got up at first dawn to hunt geese. He would not be sitting behind his desk all day, calling representatives of large distribution chains to ask if they're willing to order larger quantities of the goods he's selling. Instead, he would be coming home now to his wife and children and his little shop with 12 fat birds tied by their ankles, ready to be prepared for the eager customers that would be showing up soon. They'd always know when there was fresh fowl. No, certainly there would not have been large barns filled with chickens or pigs or cows or geese, fed on special crops to speed their growth, born and killed in captivity. There was little aid back then and man was more in contact with nature. Also, every man had the skills to grow and catch his own food. Obviously Jack would have been better at it and so he would have had a steady network of customers. As for the bathroom sink that was now filling up with lukewarm water, it would have resembled a bronze cauldron that had been boiling hot water over a fire a few minutes ago. 'That is something I would not miss', thought Jack, imagining himself burning his hands testing the water.

Let us pick up the pace of the story here and reflect on some of the changes we have created for ourselves in the last few thousand years. What Jack's story has so far illustrated is how we have created the tools and constructs to make our lives what they are today. Most of the world population no longer has to hunt or grow their own food, because we have farmers providing enough produce for entire communities. Because transportation has evolved from the occasional horse and cart to ships, trains, trucks and aeroplanes, we have come into contact with many different cultures and spices that were unknown to us in the old days and are now readily available in shops around the corner. The pepper that was almost as valuable as gold, only to be used by very rich men at exclusive banquets, is now available to all; and so it has been with many things. Whenever someone had something exclusive, we managed to find ways to get more of it more easily, making it cheaper so that demand would grow. Suddenly, what was reserved for kings only decades ago was being demanded by entire populations. The funny thing is, instead of requiring more men to satisfy the ever growing demands, we would also find ways to supply these quantities with fewer men.

One of the more recent examples is how the dawn of the industrial age brought steam engines and factories. Great weaving machines could now suddenly produce double the amount of fabric with only half the workforce. Throughout history, we have been acquiring more luxury, more diversity and more wealth, while at the same time continuously freeing members of our societies to pursue new ventures, professions and ideas. People are expected more and more to specialize in such ways that they may add value to our society. This still includes farmers, barbers, butchers and entertainers, but has also come to include professions such as (rocket) scientist, public speaker, manager and consultant. Although human societies have been growing in size, their very basic mechanisms are still there. What has changed is how we value the different aspects of our lives. Since we no longer have to worry about food, clothing and shelter, we have come to value entertainment, creativity and status as more important. If, however, we look at several nations in Africa, we can still see entire communities whose main daily concern is food.

Jack was late this morning. It is mid-winter and his car would not start, causing him to lose those precious minutes he needed to beat the traffic. Now it's 8.30am and he's stuck in traffic, on the phone to his secretary. She is giving him the telephone numbers of his 9.00am and 10.00am appointments and filling him in on the daily office news. During one particularly boring memo he received from senior management, Jack thinks fondly of his upcoming early retirement. Sometimes, leading the fast life, always having to perform according to standards, meeting targets and creating revenues, Jack feels the urge to break free of it all: 'We have made a lot of things so convenient, simple and easy that the only distinguishing aspect of our lives is the time we have to live it. And slowly, we are selling that away as well.'

Minutes later, Jack is on the phone with his first customer of the day. He is still stuck in traffic, which is particularly nasty today, and expects to make most of his morning calls in the car. His customer does not notice, as Jack is slowly convincing him in a very honeyed though business-like voice that it's surely better to reduce transportation costs by buying their full range of canned products from Jack's company. As he closes his first deal of the day, Jack cannot help but smile. He was lucky that his client, halfway across the globe, had not yet found out that one of Jack's biggest competitors had just set up shop near him.

One of the most astonishing aspects of our kind is that we use tools for almost everything, including communication. Books emerged because we wanted to transfer knowledge faster and to a wider audience than was possible by physically travelling. We needed media to hold our growing supply of information, just as speech and writing had been developed to transfer our findings to others and guard them against the passing of time. Since then, we have developed the telephone, radio, television and the internet, and because of these technologies, our circle of close friends now has a larger geographical diameter. Not only the people we know, but also the communities in which we live have grown. It is not uncommon, in fact it is quite normal, to purchase goods 'made in India' while we still consider them 'British'; think of the many companies that have set up support departments abroad nowadays, when you think you're being helped by a local representative over the phone.

The introduction of new technology is invariably met with distrust. Those who knew what came before will carefully consider the possible benefits and weaknesses of something new before fully adopting it. Over time, however, technology becomes so embedded in our daily lives, that we soon cannot live without it. Imagine a world without the telephone. Suddenly, we would be cut off from communicating with our family and friends, acquaintances and business partners. It would be impossible to verify that a certain sum of money was deposited into the bank that day. It would once again be normal to wait for several days before receiving a reply from your business partner in Sweden. Stocks would no longer be traded on a minute to minute basis, but orders would be put out for the day. The speed of information would be diminished, but also the richness of communication. You would not still be as intimate with your close buddy in Australia if you could not call him once a week and talk things over; if you had to resort to writing letters, which in itself takes longer to write than it takes to read.

We see the world of fast paced global interaction that we have created through media and communication technology and recognize we could not operate nearly as fast or be as broadly informed if we had to make do without it. In a sense, the world today would not have been possible without communications technology being available to most people. On the other hand, we consider anyone who does not use this technology as backwards or slow. Companies who do not offer support will have a lower value proposition, because we know that there are companies who can. Television stations get most of their income from advertisements because companies know that people will watch. Information density in news shows has grown because for shows to generate viewers and thus create value they will need to offer more than the morning newspaper. Employees who cannot use mobile phones will, in some lines of business, be less valuable to their employers.

It is only because we rely on the technology to perform, that we have based so many of our interactions on it. Consider 60 per cent of your letters not arriving or being answered. You would then stop writing letters and try to visit the person you wanted to correspond with. If half the time you picked up the telephone it didn't work, you would be far less inclined to pick it up. If someone has given you a mobile phone number, you expect your calls to be answered every once in a while. Back when television was unknown to us, people would restrict their interest to their local communities, with the occasional newspaper reporter coming back from abroad with an interesting story. We had to trust the information being fed to us by newspapers because only very few were able to see for themselves. We still have situations today where people would rather meet face to face because they still don't trust the telephone to accurately convey their message.

After lunch, Jack is approached by Pete, a colleague who will be taking over his job and his accounts when he retires in a month. His apprentice is not surprised by his late appearance because he had already emailed Jack's secretary to learn that he'd got stuck in traffic. It was Jack's apprentice that told him last week about the competitor setting up shop near one of his important clients. Now it's time for their daily meeting: no phone calls, no computers, just discussing clients and situations and strategies. Tomorrow, the firm demands a big presentation of the annual targets and Pete, the apprentice, has never had to deliver targets. Jack thought it would be good practice.

As they go through the numbers that Pete has come up with, it amazes Jack how much information has been dug up about the market and competitors. Apparently, with all the regulations about companies publishing annual reports and the like, the market has become a lot more transparent. *'It's all the investors' fault. If they didn't have so much information available to them, they would not be demanding so much.'* Jack frequently questions whether he still has anything of value to *teach* Pete, but each time he does, he finds something Pete has yet to *experience*.

For centuries, our economy has been driven by goods. People supplied other people with food, clothes, spices, books, livestock and so on, in exchange for other goods. Because it became very impractical to claim half a cow as payment for a dress, the concept of money came into play. Similarly, as the goods we wanted grew more complex and we needed to co-operate with others to produce them, we organized ourselves into companies. To begin with this was just a boss and some employees helping to do more of the same work to handle demand, but gradually each labourer had his own specific task and this led to people valuing and trading parts of the process leading to products. We came to recognize production factors like raw materials, labour and capital. Money in itself became distanced from the goods it represented.

In modern times most of our material needs, at least in the Western world, have been fulfilled. We all would like the latest, biggest and most luxurious car or house, but not many of us don't have a house or access to transportation. Our economies then began shifting to services. It was no longer important to offer just a product, so we began trading entire concepts behind it. A tuxedo is something to make you look good. A computer is not just a machine consuming power; it is a tool that should immediately upon purchase be able to offer you word processing and access to the internet. And so in modern economies we now have companies organizing events and functions and companies installing computer systems for you. We also have last minute rentals should someone accidentally spill wine all over your tux or service desks should your computer stop responding.

With services, it has become increasingly important not only to understand how to make a product, but also to understand how it will be put to use. Thinking of the many ways a product can be used and the possibilities of failure, allows companies to increase their service offerings. This leads businesses to demand knowledge and creativity from their workforce. They must know everything there is to know about their line of work, or be able to learn the latest facts quickly and then apply them to new ideas for creating value.

As many companies pursued value and wealth through money (words which are often confused), customers became more knowledgeable about their surroundings and companies were suddenly faced with reputations and public opinion. Not only human communities and societies, but also their subcomponents have grown. If we accept organizations, businesses and governments as components of the communities they serve, then it would also hold that their mechanisms may have changed appearance, but in their core remain the same.

Jack has had a long day at the office. At 5.00pm he called home to tell his wife he would be late, happy they had rescheduled their restaurant reservation to Saturday. It had been a long afternoon of discussion with Pete, as he had been questioning how Jack dealt with some of his accounts. Apparently, Pete had read somewhere that there were five steps to getting a client to value your company over a competitor and obviously Jack was violating two of them. The afternoon ended well after 6.00pm with both Pete and

Jack frustrated over how their company valued short-term economic gains over a sustainable service and clientele, with neither of them in the position to change very much about it. At one point in the discussion, Pete had exclaimed, *'For god's sake, we're a food selling business. Fifty years from now people will still want food. Doesn't anyone here see how stupid it is to employ hit-and-run tactics?'* Jack had to give him credit at that point, but also had to admit he was past caring; he had put in his time for the company and would soon be enjoying the life he had been working for years to secure. While driving home, Jack could think of but one thing: *'Finally, I'll have some time to enjoy myself.'*

Most of society works for some organization, with only a small percentage being true entrepreneurs. If we assume that there is still on average the same percentage of entrepreneurs among the population today as there was a century or two ago, then we must conclude that there are most likely entrepreneurs working for organizations now, instead of running them. With corporations becoming larger, even multinational, this would seem a logical conclusion: as our communities grow larger and create more room for subcommunities, it is logical that these will, in turn, come to reflect or be reflected by the larger whole.

Creativity, taking risks and seizing chances have always been the most valued human traits and those who possessed them were able to create more value and thus amass more wealth than those who did not. As change is ever more visible around us and uncertainty becoming more and more something to accept rather than avoid, organizations are looking for more flexibility, creativity and entrepreneurship in people. They push their employees to be more 'empowered', to maximize their potential, to be creative and daring, and to seize opportunities. An acronym which seems to be popping up all around us is PDP – personal development plan, in which employees state how, but most importantly that, they will develop themselves. The development of human capital, consisting of labour, knowledge but also culture, values, connections and creativity, is becoming the dominant production factor for entrepreneurs. Dealing with time and uncertainty, with change and development is becoming the dominant valued activity; this activity is learning.

As an afterthought to the story of Jack, in which we hinted at trends like globalization, virtualization, communication, technological immersion and pervasiveness, but also the need for experience, time, co-operation and stability, we have yet to discuss the concept of free time. Although most of us have condensed our working hours between Monday and Friday, 9.00am to 5.00pm, we have also chosen the same period of time for value transactions. Thank god for weekends when everyone seems to rush to shopping centres to exchange their money for the valued goods they feel they have earned. Why is it that, discounting a third of your time for when you're sleeping and another eighth for nourishing yourself, you're still considered to be useful only 44 per cent of your time; and why must we all be useful at the same time? Whoever thought up the standards of free time, working hours and job descriptions? Does free time imply that there is captivity or slavery? Do working hours imply that you are idle, unproductive or malfunctioning and under repair at other times of the day? Are job descriptions meant to restrict or empower you?

With so many things rapidly changing around us, it is also becoming increasingly important to find those things that can serve as beacons in the storm. Time is an ever more precious commodity, with so much information and so many experiences waiting to consume it, that the last thing anyone wants (and consequently the first thing anyone will try to avoid) is to be confronted with constant change just when you have finally found your place in society. At the same time, we are encouraged to change and grow into our rightful place as quickly as possible. The hardest time obviously being for those who have not found their rightful place, but are nonetheless satisfied with their achievements.

When we start looking for things to change and change comes looking for us, we will need to remember what it is we value, as individuals, as communities and organizations, as society and a species as a whole. There is often little change in our core beliefs and values, even when we are confronted with an entirely new set of circumstances, experiences and instruments. In an economic system valuing production, a doctor, who has his calling in the aid of people, may become a surgeon. Times changing, technology emerging, creativity and entrepreneurship becoming dominant economic values, an engineer, who has his calling in the aid of advancing technology to, in turn, help humans, may become a surgeon. We must learn to find the goals in what we value and how to pursue them. As we see technology, knowledge and societies expand rapidly, we must come to realize that there will always be structures and history and limits to what we do; our lesson is to be creative and ignore the obstacles.

CHAPTER 2

Meeting
Homo zappiens

❝ *In the short term, we always overstate the effects of new technologies. But in the long run, we always understate them.* **❞**

Richard Thieme

'All of a sudden, children coming into our school that year showed a quite different behaviour: direct, active, impatient, unbridled and somewhat undisciplined; it seemed to me something had happened over summer. It frightened and excited me at the same time.' This is how a Swedish teacher described her feelings when she started a new school year in the outskirts of Stockholm in the mid-1990s when six-year-old children came back to school after the summer holidays. She had the feeling that from one year to another, a new generation of children was emerging and that she had to cope with them, not yet knowing how but realizing that she would need to employ different strategies and approaches than before.

Ever since this teacher had those feelings about her students, many colleagues across Europe have experienced that students nowadays demand new approaches and teaching methods in order to keep their attention and motivation to work at school. We have heard many of them saying that students show very short attention spans, that they cannot listen for more than five minutes in the classroom. Teachers claim children cannot concentrate on one task at a time, being occupied with many things in parallel, and that students expect to get answers instantly whenever a question pops into their head. In addition, many teachers think students seem to act and think superficially, zapping from one information source to the other when watching television, surfing the internet or chatting using MSN. Children today don't seem to be critical and are even less reflective on what they digest from television and the internet.

It's not only teachers who have concerns about young children growing up in a digital world. Parents too are worried as they observe their children passing their time at home between the computer and the television screen. Parents urge their children to go and play outside, to go meet friends and engage in sports. They think that the uses of technology bring physical constraints and a poorness of social skills. In addition, parents have noticed that books no longer seem to be of interest to their children as they prefer to play computer games, including violent ones, where there seem to be no limits in moral standards.

All these concerns should be addressed if we consider the consequences of the socio-economic changes that come with the introduction of digital technology in our society. In fact, here we make a connection between children's behaviour and social context. Social behaviour never develops in a vacuum and most of our behaviour is influenced by the social context in which we have grown up. What children do and what they think is the result of the interaction with their surroundings, their outside world. And from an early age, as the world comes to them through the television, telephone and internet, the influence is important. Even more important as the world itself is changing rapidly through the revolutionizing effects of new technologies.

One of the most striking current changes is globalization. Economic globalization is leading to new developing labour markets forcing our economies to adapt to new businesses and industries. From a social point of view, however, globalization means that humans become more linked together, they become more networked. Children communicate worldwide, the internet having no limits or borders. If they play a computer game on the internet, they may communicate with anybody in the world who is willing to join them in solving a quest collaboratively or answering a question. Taking these societal changes as the background for our students' acting and thinking, let's see what exactly children are doing and what makes them so different from their parents and grandparents.

The generation that was born since the end of the 1980s has many nicknames, such as the 'net generation', 'digikids', the 'instant generation' and the 'cyber generation'. All denominations refer to specific characteristics of their surroundings or their behaviour. The net generation refers to the internet, digikids refers to the fact that children act in digital online worlds or deal with digital information. The instant generation refers to their expectation of having a response to their demands immediately. Many generations have nicknames, so why should this generation be different from others? Are differences with former generations that important or is it just another generation following the X-generation and the baby boomers? The answer is that the net generation differs more from any other past generation by the fact they have grown up in a digital era, whereas all former generations did not.

As the first ever digital natives, they have grown up in a world in which information and communication facilities are available to almost everyone and can be used in an active way. Children today spend hours a day watching television, playing computer games and chatting in chat rooms. Doing so, they process huge amounts of information through a multitude of technologies and media. They communicate with peers and others as no other generation did before, using software and devices such as television, MSN, mobile phones, iPods, blogs, Wikis, chat rooms, game consoles and other communication platforms. They use those devices and communication platforms in global technical networks, the world being their frame of reference.

Three devices have been of primary importance: the television remote control, the computer mouse and the mobile phone. With the television remote control, children have grown up choosing and watching a variety of national and foreign channels. And the number of television channels available is ever growing; via cable and satellite, children can choose any of 2,200 channels, together with 1,500 radio stations from all over the world. By watching television, children have learned to interpret images before they can even read, and to interact, albeit in a very restricted way, with a mass medium. An American study has shown that on average, 21 year olds leaving college have watched 20,000 hours of television, played over 10,000 hours' worth of computer games and have read books for 5,000 hours (Prensky, 2001). The number of hours playing computer games is increasing and, in recent surveys, the computer seems to come top of the list. Using a computer mouse, they have surfed the internet and clicked until they found whatever they wanted, looking for icons, sounds and movements rather than characters. The mobile phone has helped them to communicate with their mum and friends at their convenience, since physical distance does not present any means of communication restriction.

The uses of these technologies have influenced *Homo zappiens'* thinking and behaviour. To them, most of the information they are looking for is only a click away, as is anybody they want to contact. They hold a positive view on their possibilities of getting the right information at the right time from anybody or anywhere. They learn at a very early stage that there are many information sources and that these may claim various truths. They practise in filtering information and learn to make up their minds in networks of peers with whom they communicate frequently. School does not seem to have that much influence on their attitudes and values. We will call this generation *Homo zappiens*, a seemingly new species that acts in a global cyber culture relying on multimedia. How do they act and how do they develop their behaviour as we can observe it? Let's look at three typical situations most parents will be acquainted with.

The first one is an ordinary school day when students hang around at the school gates waiting for the bus to come or taking their bikes to go home. Once home, they start up their computer and begin a MSN conversation with the very same classmates they have just left at school. They play online games together and other friends whom they have accepted into their MSN contact list also join in. Their MSN contact list is full with up to 150 contacts, as MSN does not allow users to have more.[1] A national Microsoft survey has shown that the average number of conversations that children deal with when using MSN is about ten, and they manage to have these conversations while clicking from one screen to the other, a coloured and blinking toolbar alerting them to the fact there is a response waiting for them.

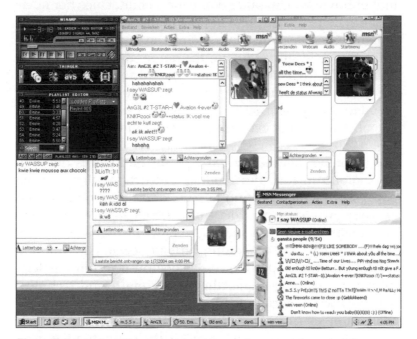

Figure 2.1 A typical *Homo zappiens'* computer screen in use while chatting

---

[1] With MSN 7.0, the capacity for contacts has been expanded from 150 to 300.

Some of the contacts are blocked: a kid not willing to communicate with somebody for a while or forever. They have strict rules. If you pose as another person in MSN you will be blocked and excluded from communication. The idea is that you are in control of with whom you have conversations and about what and when. Conversations can easily be closed at any time. Just write: 'CU' (see you), 'l8r' (later) or nothing at all, and click on the X symbol in the upper right corner of your screen since there are no formalities as existed before. MSN is currently one of the most common communication platforms used. In the Netherlands alone there are four million users (almost a quarter of the population), sending 22 million messages a day.[2] MSN is almost always on – *Homo zappiens* are networked with virtual as well as physical friends.

The second situation that many parents will recognize is that of buying a computer game for a child. Once home, he or she is eager to start playing the game, and loads the disc into the computer. You start reading the instruction manual, while the child starts playing the game. By the time you're on page 11, the child is probably already well underway in the game. And when they get stuck, they simply phone a friend to ask for help, surf a cheat website or ask someone at school. They do not even consider reading the instructions.

The difference between *Homo zappiens* and you is that you work along linear lines reading instructions first – using paper ware – then starting to play, and figuring out things on your own when you get stuck. *Homo zappiens* do it the non-linear way, by first starting to play the game, and then, should they get stuck, phoning a friend, seeking information on the internet or posting a message on a forum for help. Instead of working alone, they use human and technical networks when needed for instant replies. This is why the generation of *Homo zappiens* has been called the instant generation. They want answers to their questions almost instantly, which has become a reality for most of them. *Homo zappiens* have experienced ways of getting instant

[2] Nielsen/Netratings: MSN populairste IM in Europa, 18 March 2004, www.emerce.nl/nieuws.jsp?id=254476

answers if you simply submit your question to the right person, forum, chat room or discussion board.

The third situation that most parents will be familiar with is *Homo zappiens* watching television. Zapping channels is common as most children watch up to six or more channels simultaneously. All of them do so, and it has become rare for a child to just watch one channel for more than an hour. Music channels, such as MTV, are popular but are mixed with other channels at a time. Parents may worry about this behaviour as zapping seems to occur randomly or at least at moments when their children get bored. In addition, it is hard to watch television together when one of the family members holds the remote control for zapping. As a consequence, many children today have television sets in their rooms, and often have them on while playing computer games. Here again, the difference between you and *Homo zappiens* is that you have been trained to watch one channel at a time, not even having the opportunity to switch when you were young. The zap culture of *Homo zappiens* upsets parents because they think children do not get the messages from various programmes and as a consequence their knowledge becomes rather shallow.

When doing their homework for school, *Homo zappiens* also do different things at the same time. While doing their homework, children are listening to their favourite music using a CD or MP3 player, answering MSN messages, and if they have a television in their room, it's likely to be switched on. The old rule of doing one thing at a time and 'you will do it right', does not apply anymore to this generation. They divide their attention between the different incoming signals and decide to process them if appropriate, varying their level of attention according to their timely interest. If the television is broadcasting a popular clip, the child 'switches on' its attention for this information source; after that the attention level is lowered as other clips that are less interesting pass by.

Doing their homework for school is a matter of last minute planning. Whereas you learned to plan your homework well in advance, *Homo zappiens* start work at the latest possible moment. School is just a part of their lives; it's not the main activity. They know they have to attend school and take their exams but for these children school appears to be a meeting place for friends, a social space, rather than a place to learn. It is the place where you physically talk to your friends, a place where you network. They will do their homework using their networks and finish just in time to hand in their work. If you've been to college, you will probably recall similar behaviour; however, at primary or secondary school, planning your homework and so on, was more of a habit that was trained and was more common among students.

Wikipedia, online collaborative effort in knowledge gathering

Wikipedia is an online encyclopedia initiative. It is an application and example of social software: the platform offers a means of joint community word-processing, in this case creating the world's largest free encyclopedia. The name is based on the term 'wiki wiki', which is Hawaiian for 'quick'. A wiki is a type of website that allows visitors to quickly add or edit content. The technology can be used to create works of online collaboration, constantly updated by anyone who feels the need to.

Wikipedia offers a treasury of contemporary encyclopedia articles on a wide range of subjects. As with any encyclopedia, it's not and may never be 'complete' but one of the biggest advantages is that it can be updated constantly by over six billion potential internet users. If there is something not in the wikipedia, you are free to add it yourself.

As with other community efforts, Wikipedia thrives on trust. If someone decides to write an article that, for example, the Holocaust never happened, this may be found on Wikipedia. It is then up to the community to correct the error. This, by default, ensures that the content in the encyclopedia reflects what the majority of active users view as the truth. To edit an article you have to create an identity, so changes can be traced back, although it's also permitted to anonymously submit information for acceptance. Articles that the community values highly may be awarded a 'featured article' position, which is the equivalent, for example, of a high rating in a Google search result.

Instead of appointing experts in different fields of science, social structures, languages and so on, who then form authorities which provide the community with information, Wikipedia provides an alternative approach that may be much quicker in supplying the community with the information they require. Instead of looking for the right people to supply you with information, you could ask an entire community to throw together their collective knowledge. If the topic is interesting enough, you will have a short response time and many individuals may add tiny morsels of information, which together may give you the answer you need or even point you to an answer you never considered.

On the other hand, suppose you think that the life and death of an elder statesman is so interesting that anyone should at least be able to gain access to this information from a reputed source. Why wait for the editor of the Britannica to approve the value of your submission, when you can publish the information to an entire community and have those who think it interesting decide whether the information has relevance to them? If we decided that the term, as well as the title of this book, *'Homo zappiens'* is worth an article on Wikipedia, we might write such an article and place it there.

Homo zappiens live in a world of rich information resources. Lindström and Seybold (2003) stated that a child nowadays absorbs about 8,000 brand images or logos a day. Such an information load seems a burden for many parents and all those who were born before the 1980s, but *Homo zappiens* do not seem to have a problem in processing huge amounts of information. They have embraced computer and media technology as former generations did electricity; information and communication technology has become an integral part of their life. Amazingly, they have become at ease with computers on their own and without taking courses; they manipulate their mobile phones sending SMS messages using their two thumbs or just one if the other hand is not free, and they have expertise downloading and modifying music files, utility software such as compressing tools, and programming tools.

However, these skills do not mean they are all 'techies'; only some of them are interested in programming or informatics. Most of them do not show a particular interest in technology itself, they just use it. If they need to use a tool, such as LimeWire or WinRAR, they know how to download, install and use it to send music files. If, however, the standard installation procedures present them with technical problems, most of them will blame the technology. And if their friends cannot help them solve the problem, they will probably uninstall the program and simply try installing another one. Technology is there to serve them; if it does not it is the technology that fails.

Former generations tend to consider technology as something difficult to master, video recorders being notorious devices that were impossible to handle. Sending SMS messages is still problematic for most parents, and of course computers are still user unfriendly for quite a large percentage of people, although we would not like to neglect all those who have battled their way into the digital age. *Homo zappiens*, however, treat technology as a friend and with every new device that emerges on the market, question how the new gadget could help them do what they want better or quicker. For them, the ultimate criteria for adopting technology is not the user friendliness of it, but the opportunity of its serving their demands and needs.

In fact, *Homo zappiens* were born with a computer mouse in their hand, were able to manipulate the television remote control from the age of three and had a mobile phone at eight years old. And the uses of technology don't stop there; CD Walkmans, iPods, MP3 players, digital cameras, Xboxes, GameCubes, and PlayStations 2 and 3, help them to become more dexterous and skilful with technology.

What's so important about using all of these devices? Is it only about the skills they develop by handling them? Or does the influence of using technology stretch beyond operational skills? The answer may well be affirmative. All of the above mentioned devices have something crucial in common: they give the user control of a wide variety of information flows and communication. Any user can, at any moment, activate, switch or stop these devices by simply clicking a button. They put users in a controlling position of deciding which information to process or which communication to engage in or not. They do not only enable the user to keep control of information flows, they also help them deal with information overload, and to select the information efficiently, properly, swiftly and according to their needs. *Homo zappiens'* speed of using the internet to look for information is high and to parents, it might seem a matter of pure chance that they find what they want. Only if you search for Information together with a child will they show you the contrary. It is a matter of skill, not at all a matter of chance. Their searching skills are much higher than ours and it's unlikely you'll be able to catch up with them even after having practised for a long time.

Homo zappiens have developed skills for selecting false or true information from the internet. It is striking to see that they recognize websites, in particular, weblogs in which girls or boys present themselves and their daily life and activities, but in fact the whole site or blog is just an ad for a company. Through hidden clues such as specific products that are represented in web pages, children distinguish 'ad-sites' and learn to detect information's purposes. By the very information overload they have to cope with, they develop expertise in valuing information, making themselves less vulnerable for indoctrination or misleading messages.

New technologies are predominant in their lives, in particular multimedia interactive computer applications, such as computer games. Most youngsters start playing games from the age of three onwards. Simple games are available in many shops today and before a child goes to nursery school, it has learned the first principles of maths, it can recognize rectangular, circular and pyramidal forms and figures, it knows how to pay for goods in a shop, how to rank or bring objects together, and it knows how to use a computer and manipulate the keyboard. For *Homo zappiens*, learning starts with play and it is an exploratory play as they discover and proceed in a game.

These simple games meant for early childhood address boys and girls alike. At this stage there is no gender issue. As children grow up boys have shown to be more interested in violent games or war-oriented games. Shoot' em up games have not been the preferred environments for girls in the first place. Initially, they have been more focused on puzzle and adventure games, and they have been most active in applications related to communication. But gender differences are slowly fading away as girls' participation in multiplayer internet games appears to progress steadily. In those internet games both violence and strategic thinking are closely interlinked and thus provide environments where not only mere 'force and destruction' seem to reign. We should add here that in games, such as Counter Strike or Grand Theft Auto, it might seem that the violence aspect appeals to boys, but in fact it is something different which attracts them to play these games. For boys, violence is not the ultimate goal; what really attracts them is the agility and the ability to react or respond to sudden situations. What parents see their children play is the so-called declarative layer of the game, which is all you see on the computer screen. However, underneath this computer screen lays the engine of the game. Just as Monopoly has become famous as a game related to money making, the very same engine laying underneath Monopoly has been used for building many other declarative layers, and thus, many other games.

As girls tend to play more 'violent' games nowadays, boys tend to use more communication tools. These tools started with chat rooms, MSN, ICQ and other facilities, but recently new tools have become available, such as profile sites, services such as You Tubes, Hives, Google Video Blog and other free internet environments where you can show and share not only written information about yourself, but also audio-visuals with digital cameras now available to many at low cost. Although the gender issue has been apparent during the take off phase of gaming, we expect *Homo zappiens* to use technology independently from gender. In addition, if we look at the underlying principles of games and communication environments those principles appear not to be that gender specific. And this is the reason the gender issue of technology will probably be a temporary issue.

Some time ago, a student teacher working in my research group carried out a practical experiment, asking five-year-old children to create a fantasy story. One of the girls made two drawings, and then asked her teacher if she could use her digital camera. She took digital pictures of her drawings, and then started to make a photo strip, taking pictures of her bear that was going to be her guest star, baking eggs, eating them and going to sleep. She then put all the pictures into a PowerPoint presentation, adding dialogue over the images to help tell her story. She asked her teacher to help her with dubbing the sound and writing the subtitles that she dictated. After one hour, she presented her story to the classroom and many of her peers liked her presentation so much that they also presented her story over and over again. This five-year-old girl was not a gifted child or had any specific talent; she was an ordinary child in an ordinary school. She had simply grown up with technology.

Homo zappiens spend a lot of hours playing computer games. If parents do not set a fixed number of hours per day for using the computer and watching television, children seem to have no limits. Playing outside is of no interest to them, although parents try to force them to go out as much as they possibly can. Children play a variety of computer games: first person shooting games, adventure games, role-playing games and many others. Children play games on game consoles, on the computer and on small portable devices, and they have their preferences for specific games and devices. They talk a lot about games with their peers and it seems to be the most popular topic for discussions, together with music clips and films, such as those of *Harry Potter*, *Sin City*, *The Matrix Reloaded* or *The Lord of the Rings*.

Since the 1980s, computer games have become tougher to play, there are complex problems and puzzles to solve and the roles you can take up are far more elaborate than a decade ago. Nonetheless, children continue to play them and find a challenge in doing so. Why? Why do children spend hours and hours to get to level 35 in the World of Warcraft? Why do they want to become that skilled orc or paladin and even pay for it on a monthly basis? The World of Warcraft is a multiplayer internet game that has developed over ten years from a single player CD-ROM game into a global game on the internet where currently more than three million people pay to play.

Several issues may explain the perseverance of children to play difficult computer games. First, whatever type of game they play, children have to be *active* from the beginning. Games do not have introductory explanations on how you should play it or how to start it, although there might be an exercise module in some of them. Secondly, games are demanding and challenging players to take the reins and be *in control*, find out by themselves and help themselves. As a consequence, *Homo zappiens* learn very quickly to find their way through. At a very early age, they still ask their parents how to start up games. But parents are soon surpassed by their children and from the age of seven or eight, children no longer need the help of their parents. Thirdly, children become *immersed* in computer games – taking on the personality of the role they are playing and acting according to its characteristics. Players get consumed in a virtual world, making it a real world for the time they are playing. These three characteristics of gaming – being active, being in control and being immersed – are crucial for their motivation to continue playing really complicated games.

Playing games can become a socially intense happening when children decide to organize a LAN (local area network) party. Friends come together, each of them bringing their computer or laptop along.

Figure 2.2 Children conducting a LAN party

Most LAN party attendees are boys, aged from 14 up to 22 or even 26, from various backgrounds, various school types, knowing each other from other parties or occasions. One of the systems is configured as the server for the network and all computers are organized in a local area network on which they can play games together. They form groups collaborating or competing with each other or everyone plays against the computer itself, and if they are playing a multiplayer internet game, virtual gamers join the party. The atmosphere is a bit like a simultaneous chess party, but much more informal, and more collaborative. Players talk about strategies they think are most effective; there are long periods of silence too where everybody is highly concentrated. LAN parties last for at least 36 to 48 hours without sleeping. I have assisted in several LAN parties and must say that it's exhausting. But when you get tired, you just lay down for an hour or two on a couch. I can recommend that every parent and grown-up should attend a LAN party at least once; it's certainly an education! Being invited to join and to watch children playing those games is a real pleasure, and provides a great opportunity to communicate with them and get a better understanding of their behaviour, attitudes and beliefs.

The need for control is also apparent when *Homo zappiens* play games in the school playground. Instead of playing games according to fixed rules, children like to invent their own games and set their own rules. Many of these games have neither winners nor losers. Game rules are there to be changed, that is the fun, and as a consequence, a game is an evolving social event steered by the players.

The *Homo zappiens* generation uses technology '24/7'. MSN is always on; talking to friends is just one or two clicks away. Recently, a teacher told me of his experiences during a school camp at the beginning of the school year. Before the age of the mobile phone, his students came up to him to discuss problems they encountered during the camp. Nowadays, nobody comes to see him with a problem; they phone their mum or dad and discuss with them how to solve it. *Homo zappiens* live in a networked world and this world is not restricted to the traditional boundaries of the town or country they live in. Networks are human and technological. Their human networks are those used for interpersonal communication, albeit physical or virtual.

Technical networks consist of technical infrastructures (mainly the internet), computers, devices and software that they use for storing and retrieving information. Their human networks include those people they talk to through MSN, chat rooms, mail facilities, school or just at the sports club. A characteristic of *Homo zappiens* is that they easily integrate virtual friends and physical neighbours. Physically being there or not does not seem to make a difference to them. They can play multiplayer games on the internet and collaborate within a team consisting of individuals that they've never met, and will never meet physically. They do not feel the need to know somebody physically before they can work together. In the multiplayer internet game World of Warcraft, you will meet avatars, representations of players somewhere in the world. With some of them, you may collaborate in solving a quest, such as conquering a huge monster in some dark cave, in order to find keys needed to progress in the game.

Figure 2.3 The main portal to World of Warcraft, a popular MMO(RP)G

The World of Warcraft game requires that you link up with peers to penetrate the cave under penalty of not surviving if you enter on your own. I've played in such quests with other players completely unknown to me and we communicated via a chat facility about our strategy for the game. Once we accomplished our mission, each of us continued on his own path but it was fun to work together and we even exchanged some funny information about ourselves. Frequent players of the World of Warcraft create guilds; groups of mostly experienced children and adults collaborating in solving major quests. They communicate using tools such as Ventrillo and Teamspeak, chat and audio tools enabling them to write and talk via the internet.

Children apply similar approaches in searching and uploading information on the internet. It is no longer only words they put on the internet, cyber culture is multimedia oriented. Communicating with images is an approach that *Homo zappiens* prefer to use. Tell what you want to say by sending an image. Put your images on the internet and share them with others. Flickr.com is an example of so-called social software and an online service where people from all over the world are uploading their digital pictures, and sharing them with each other. It's up to users to decide to whom they give access to their pictures and whether to allow others to add 'tags'. Tags are keywords that you attach to your images helping people to search and find your pictures more easily.

There is a multitude of facilities available for users, varying from simple up- and downloading to creating public and private blogs, and tools for manipulating images. If you've been to a wedding with friends and family, it's possible to upload your photos in a private area and indeed to share all the photos that people took during the special day. The most appealing feature of Flickr.com is that anyone can add tags with comments to any of the photos. As all the pictures are digital, you can use them in conjunction with many software tools that allow you to manipulate the image.

The internet is just as real as the living room or school. It's a meeting place, a social cyberspace. That is why blogs have become popular among younger people. Blogs are digital diaries accessible to everyone. You can put in anything, stories, your beliefs, your experiences, photos, games, whatever you want to share with the outside world. The difference with an ordinary website is that blogs offer facilities for communication with readers, friends, colleagues or anybody who would like to contact you. Blogging changes the view on the concept of privacy. What information is sharable with others appears to move along with technology coming into our lives. Although it must be said that technology is an enabling technology, we must also recognize that it does influence the openness in our society and as a consequence the way we tend to think about concepts such as privacy.

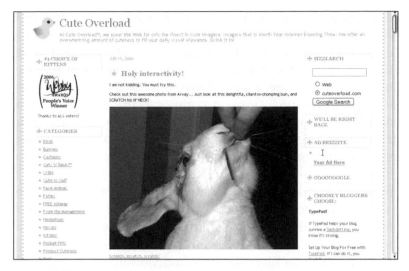

Figure 2.4 A blog on the cutest imagery to be found on the internet

A good example of changing concepts of privacy is the '43 Things' website (www.43things.com). In '43 Things' both children and adults describe their wishes and ambitions for the short and long term. If you visit the home page, you will see the different wishes listed in a 'tag cloud', the very popular ones in bigger letters, the less popular in minor script. Clicking on the tags leads you to the participating individuals connected to that tag. You can immediately start participating in the community by adding, commenting or submitting questions. Individuals share very private information on the site, such as their anxieties, their health issues and way of life. One of the tags I looked at was 'stop cutting', where I found pictures of participants showing the results of self-inflicted cuts to their bodies. They formed a community to discuss their problems in a very open way, something much more difficult to realize face to face.

Browsing these internet environments you discover that people of all social classes participate in these virtual communities. The internet is no longer an environment of social exclusion. On the contrary, the internet brings people together from all socio-economic backgrounds. And although in the past it might have been an issue that low income families were unable to spend money on having a computer and internet connection at home, the number of households who have is ever increasing. Internet environments, such as '43 Things', show that the internet is a place for everyone, not just the middle classes. Of course, the fact still exists that not everyone can afford to buy the necessary hardware, and so forth, but the issue is no longer if you can afford to have a computer, the issue is having access to technology. Schools, libraries, internet cafés and other public places are currently providing services to access the internet and participate in virtual communities. The digital divide in the first and second world is no longer a matter of socio-economic classes, rather a generation issue; older people not connected to virtual realities, thinking that technologies are only for techies, and as a consequence, not seeing the opportunities and the major socio-economic changes, such as globalization, individualization and new technologies, occurring in our societies.

On a global level, however, there still exists the digital divide in the traditional sense, poverty preventing access to knowledge and communication through technology. This is an issue that does not stand on its own; it's embedded in the most important challenge we have to address this century. Equal division of wealth among nations is what must be achieved, under penalty of serious revolutions or wars. Technology is not to blame here; on the contrary technology provides huge opportunities to contribute to level this global digital divide. There are already great initiatives: Wikipedia the free online encyclopedia meant to serve the developing world; and the '75 Euro computer', a cheap computer, fit to serve in less wealthy countries with restricted electricity networks. This computer is currently in production and will be widely available in the near future. But let's come back to *Homo zappiens*' behaviour.

Flickr, the community way of sharing imagery

Fully in line with the efforts to create communities on the internet and make sharing of resources among them easier, Flickr is a site where users can maintain an online database of their photos. Each photo uploaded and added to the site can be traced back to the user's account and there's also the ability for any user who views the picture to attach their comments, as well as to sort photos into categories (sets).

Users of Flickr may add stories to their pictures, thus explaining what can be seen in the picture, or add a funny interpretation of an image. Visitors may also comment on the many other aspects of an image.

Efforts such as Flickr are interesting. People share experiences and art, photos and stories much like the artists of old. In the future, Flickr may host one of the biggest digital galleries of this century.

What is of further interest to note is that Flickr mainly uses the 'Creative Commons' methods of protecting intellectual property rights. As an alternative to traditional 'all rights reserved' copyrighting, Creative Commons joins in with the internet community movement and offers 'some rights reserved' copyright. As information is more and more becoming a free-for-all commodity, with cost free alternatives arising almost as soon as someone starts attaching a fee to a bit of knowledge, it makes more sense to merely restrict rights than deny them. True value is no longer in the information, but in the level of trust and use a particular piece of information receives. Information cannot be trusted or used if you deny access. For a complete review of Creative Commons and the services this organization provides to the internet community, visit http://creativecommons.org.

By using the internet, children have learned how to search and find information they need and by playing computer games, such as Civilization III, Grand Theft Auto or World of Warcraft, they *learn by discovery and by experimenting*. They can experiment freely; the computer provides the opportunity to start over and over again. It never punishes or is condescending. When you fail to reach the level you want and lose your final life, the game flashes a 'game over' message and you can start again. If they don't want to start all over again, they can simply cheat and use a code they've found on the internet. In most computer games, you can make yourself invulnerable by getting an unlimited amount of lives. It is interesting to see that many children use cheats to get through the game for the first time. But when they finish, they return to the level they could not solve on their own and start the game again without cheats!

What you learn in a computer game can be practised over and over again, the lack of punishment giving a strong feeling of confidence and self-esteem. It makes you confident of being able to address a problem that seems complicated and complex. Once the problem is solved, they experience a positive feedback and this helps them to be even more motivated for the next challenge. Since *Homo zappiens* are networked persons, they use their networks for solving problems. With a little help from your peers, you can achieve levels that you couldn't before. By phoning or MSN-ing a friend, children learn collaboratively, exchange their strategies and give each other hints on how to play better. The feeling of 'we' is stronger than the feeling of 'me'.

Computer games are so appealing to children it's as if game developers have cracked how to keep them motivated and focused on the challenges within the game. When asking children what is so attractive about the games, they say it's not so much the element of fun that's important. Fun is OK, of course, but it's not the primary reason for their engagement in games. It's the challenge that attracts them to play; being challenged to succeed in solving a problem and getting to the next level. Without wanting to offend many good colleagues, I dare say that game developers have understood the psychology of students better than many educationalists. If we could only use their strategies in schools! By playing computer games, *Homo zappiens* have become active processors of information, and skilled problem solvers, developing problem-solving strategies.

Using a multitude of communication devices, *Homo zappiens* have also become effective communicators. There are hardly any barriers for them to phone, Skype, MSN or email a friend, and most of the time communications are kept short. Using SMS language has become second nature even when they talk on the phone. Although informal, SMS language has become a way of communication for which dictionaries are now available on the internet. Many fundamental readings can also be found in SMS language on the internet. The European Constitution can be read in SMS language and even the Bible has been translated into SMS language.

Technology has shaped their way of being, they think in networks and in collaboration more than former generations did. They rely on technology as a friend not as a foe (Prensky, 2002). Their way of being is digital rather than analogue. And their learning strategies have changed accordingly, if we accept that by playing games and by communicating with others children do learn. We will come to this relationship between using technology and learning in the next chapter.

As mentioned before, *Homo zappiens* consider school as a meeting place for friends rather than a learning environment. School does not challenge them sufficiently for learning and is currently at risk of getting disconnected from its audience. School is one of the focal points for students' daily life, but it's not the most important one. It's as if school stands apart from their lives, another world completely different from the rest of their daily contacts and activities. A school director of a secondary school recently talked to his son who had just finished school and decided to enrol in a university course. He said: '*Well dad, it's not the school building that's wrong, nor the teachers. Many of them try to do their best and are quite OK. But what is wrong is that school is so dull, the content, the curriculum, really sucks.*' If you listen to children, you will hear them say these kinds of things. We thought, as educationalists, we had developed, carefully and deliberately, a curriculum that was relevant and preparatory for further education. And although we knew, by our own experience, that much of the content we learned at school did not serve us that well during our lives, we still consider our national curricula relevant. Children today think differently and say the content is irrelevant for their further lives, and even for their studies. Should we listen and start thinking differently about the necessity of a standardized curriculum for all?

In addition to the issue of content, 'chalk and talk' classrooms are not appealing to *Homo zappiens*. It simply contrasts too much with their way of working. The contrast with their out of school life is too big: no control, no connectivity, no media, no action, no immersion and no networks. As a learner in school they feel forced to be passive and listen to a teacher who explains. In most schools, it's even forbidden to have your phone switched on, even when the sound is off! So, what you do is send SMS messages hiding your phone under your table, while 'listening' to the teacher, looking at him as if you were interested and nodding from time to time. You can find the buttons easily as the 5 key has a little dot on it for blind writing. In many school media centres students do not have the right to use MSN or to visit websites that are not explicitly related to education.

To conclude this chapter, schools and parents tend to look at children from the point of view of what they think children *should do* according to their values and norms. There is nothing wrong with that, all generations have done it – we call it raising children – however, since this generation is the first generation that teaches their parents how to use a forum, how to use a mobile phone, and to do their telebanking and other online bookings, this is the first time we can observe 'inverse education' taking place, a phenomenon never seen before. Because of these major changes in our society, parents and teachers should observe children in what they *actually do* and try to understand that this generation will live in a different world for which new skills, attitudes and behaviours are compulsory.

Many parents and teachers, however, are convinced that playing computer games, chatting on the internet and zapping television stations is a waste of time. Some of them probably think that the only positive side effect of playing games is that you develop good hand-eye co-ordination. But most of them do not see that playing computer games helps learning. As far as we are concerned, by using the internet, playing computer games and zapping television channels, children actually develop valuable skills that go beyond instrumental skills, such as hand-eye co-ordination. In the next chapter, we will try to show how *Homo zappiens* develop learning skills that are critical for learning and extremely useful in an information society in which it is no longer the content that matters. We would also like to talk about the relation between learning and the uses of technology, and make some connections between learning in our future society, where we will increasingly depend on creativity, attention and knowledge as prime assets for survival.

DSpace, a flexible, customizable, innovative resource storage system

D SPACE

Welcome to DSpace

DSpace is a digital repository software system developed to aid the academic community in the management and archiving of now increasingly digital material. It is the underlying infrastructure on which an interface, such as E-trax (see page 93) may function; indeed they both share some of the same functionality and design principles. DSpace is an effort to create the digital library of tomorrow with the current best practices of community networking efforts.

Imagine you have a system that will take any type of media and content you can throw at it – video, pictures, journals, hyperlinks, book-scans, digital texts, online tests. Imagine it will allow you to upload these onto a system with an ease of use and support of standards not yet often seen, especially in free software! Such a system would allow you to reuse your material for different courses, presentations, books, readers and interviews without having to duplicate it several times. You would just send whoever is interested to the repository and let them search by keywords to find the desired material.

For the coming decades, it will be increasingly important that users can maintain control of their information flows and resources with the same speed and ease of use with which one can search the internet. When you finish writing a report, you want to catalogue it online in your own library system with the possibility for those interested to easily find it. You want the system not to be bothered whether you upload a file as a Word document, Acrobat file or PowerPoint presentation. You don't want to have to make six copies of the same collection of articles into a system, just because you happen to be teaching six courses in which this text is used. You want the system to be online, so you, as well as those you permit, can access your resources from anywhere. Actually, you may want to consider whether you want to restrict your resources from certain people at all.

Making sense of chaos

> *What is best about the best games is that they draw kids into some very hard learning.*
>
> Seymour Papert

How can we interpret children's use of technology? Is their seemingly chaotic behaviour of zapping between television channels and surfing the internet a matter of wasting time? Is watching television and playing computer games useful in some sense? Or do the benefits of playing games or surfing the internet simply stop at developing an advanced level of hand-eye co-ordination? As far as the latter skill is concerned, it appears that young surgeons who have played computer games during their childhood perform better in surgery than those who have not (Rosser, 2004). Of course, you could argue that only a small part of our labour force will go on to become surgeons, so the advantages of a well developed hand-eye co-ordination applies only to a restricted number of professions. So how then could technology help the majority to take advantage of the uses of technology? To what extent can technology help children to become better learners?

On a Saturday morning around 10.00am, a group of ten friends (varying in age from 14 to 27) comes together at my place for a LAN party that will last for 31 hours. A LAN party is a meeting of children and adults where they play computer games without any sleep, unless you feel that tired that you have to take a nap on the couch for an hour or two. Most of the gamers will be boys – girls are a definite minority; only two will participate. The group consists of individuals of mixed abilities, varying from lower vocational to higher secondary and university level. The participants have arranged the meeting in advance and tasks have been divided, ensuring that there will be one computer to function as the server and that everyone will bring their own computer or laptop.

Collaboratively, the gamers arrange tables and chairs to set up the computers in such a way that you can get as many of them on a square metre as is physically possible. Within an hour the intranet is working, most of the systems are connected, and all the computer games they intend to play have been installed and configured for the intranet. I notice that the youngest child actually did the technical work; the older players just plugged their systems into the intranet. I also notice that school type does not seem to be relevant for the skills of setting up the network. Those in lower vocational training appear to be leading here. There is some initial discussion about what game to play. This weekend the main game will be Counter Strike, a game that you can play against the computer, against others or with a friend against others. All these possibilities will be tried out. It appeals that you can game with one of your friends and go and fight two others. But it's even more challenging to compete with the computer and play against it collaboratively. They start playing around noon. Surprisingly, most of the time there is no music playing.

Although each player has earphones on, most of the time they seem to be discussing tactics, giving advice on how to tackle a problem or just having fun about their successes or losses. There are, however, long hours without any sound – children concentrating on the game being played as if their lives depended on it. Food and beverages consist mainly of Coca-Cola and crisps. At 6.00am, some friends drop in on their way home from a party. Those that are tired take a rest for an hour and the friends who have dropped by take over their computers for a while. After an hour or two playing, they have some drinks and then leave; the LAN party continues until 5.00pm. The rhythm starts to slow down, as most of the children discuss their results. Some diehards are still busy trying to reach the next level but I am very happy to be going to bed.

Compared with LAN parties, it's far more relaxing to watch interrupted snippets of various television programmes when children are zapping channels. Whereas my activities at a LAN party have been more of a participative observer, the role I had while watching television with children has been one of an interviewer. Many times when children have changed channels I ask them why. Most of the time their answers are short, and it took a while before I could find a pattern in their zapping behaviour.

Watching children's behaviour and talking to them frequently, I've found that they do not act without any purpose or just for fun. Maybe, the most important mind shift I have made comes from playing computer games and zapping television channels. By interacting with technology in the same way that children do, I have changed my view on what can be learned from computer games, mobile phones, MSN and zapping between television channels. I have come to understand what authors, such as James Paul Gee, Sherry Turkle, Wolf and Perron, Goodson and Lankshear, Oblinger and Oblinger and many other researchers have tried to show about the relationships between playing and learning and the role of technology in children's lives. On the basis of my observations, I have discerned a number of skills that children develop from using technology, and it's my opinion that these skills also relate to learning. I will describe these below.

Iconic skills

Children surf the internet intensively and have been introduced to a world of multimedia where every screen they see is full colour, has multiple images, often with sound and movement, such as blinking icons, and, of course, text. Texts are usually short since web pages are not configured for long readings. Words are often underlined, providing links, known as hyperlinks, to relevant pages or other pop-up windows. Their strategies for finding information in this multimedia world differ from how you were taught to source information. Searching for information together with children taught me that, most of the time, I was slower than them.

The difference between them and me is that when I look at a web page, I can hardly stop my eyes from trying to find information as if I was reading. My eyes tend to look at the upper left corner of the screen and search for words to read that can help me to continue finding my way around that particular website. My behaviour is easily explained as, for decades, I have been trained to read printed matter that consisted of only two colours in the form of semantic characters, just like this book! I've also discovered that my second strategy of scanning texts is like going through newspaper headings. Sometimes this works, but this strategy ignores colours, icons, pictures, movements and sounds. And these are omnipresent in web pages.

As a consequence, my generation is much more focused on semantic symbols. Contrarily, children are less so and proceed differently in clicking and surfing the internet. They incorporate the symbols and icons on the screen in their search for information. They have come to know the meaning of a variety of icons, recognizable in different environments, all of which tell them quickly where to go. They have learned that icons and symbols have information value and are functional when processing information, and that colours also have similar added value. A colour has an informational meaning and so is an appropriate tool for recognizing or categorizing information.

My generation has grown up with just black on white characters in an age where colours were used for embellishment and illustration. *Homo zappiens* have learned to use many more signals to search for information than only characters, and in a multimedia future it will be a mandatory skill to deal with this iconic information next to the traditional textual symbols.

Blogs, the online column with interactivity and multimedia

Weblogging is becoming increasingly more popular among internet users. What used to be a personal website, giving you a small corner on the internet to call your own, has now become a weblog, or 'blog' for short. It is a personal website, with links to others' sites, offering video, audio, photos, podcasts and personal articles, along with the means to provide a forum and comment on most items in the blog. It's like a personal diary, which can be read by everyone and added to, although the creator can still maintain some form of veto.

Aside from diaries, blogs are also used, for example, for current world affairs, discussing specific topics, journalism in general and to expand on existing websites. The new generation of internet users is increasingly using the internet to form communities and networks in which they discuss anything. They rely on these communities to provide them with relevant information and use these communities to vent their ideas, for peer discussion and review, as well as feedback on what information is relevant.

Consider a community of people interested in learning. They may be organized around a few blogs. Every week, a few highly regarded experts from this community write some additions to the community blogs, whereafter people comment on these ideas and may add their own views or links to other interesting materials. It's like sharing your daily views on the world with your academic colleagues and then discussing over coffee how to deal with them.

What the new generation of internet users is coming to understand is that you need to participate in networks, to both give and receive in order to maintain the networks that are so beneficial to generating knowledge, digesting information and negotiating values. These new users immerse themselves in the electronic world with abandon, creating as much of an online identity as they can, so that their virtual selves blend in and mirror their real-life persona. Why fear the world, when you can dive in, take part and enjoy?

If you want to create your own blog, it's easy to do so. Just pick one of the many sites offering you a small space to place your information, often paid for by advertisement banners that will be displayed around your blog. Alternatively, with more in-depth software knowledge, you can download templates and create your own custom blog on a rented web space, possibly provided by your ISP (internet service provider) as part of your subscription.

Alternatively, search for a blog on a topic of your interest and find a (small) community maintaining a discussion around persons, items or subjects of your interest. Leave a remark and enter into a, possibly lively, discussion with the author(s) of the blog. No longer need you read a book and learn of ideas that may have already become outdated since their printing. Blogs are like new books, containing the mobile phone number of the author with the comment, 'call me'.

As information will continue to grow exponentially in the present century, children today need to have the skills to deal with huge amounts of information, with the ability to skim and select swiftly in many instances. If not, they risk being overloaded and have no time to go into detail for those information resources that must be studied and reflected upon in more depth. Parents worry sometimes about the way their children surf the internet, downloading, copying and pasting information, not seeming to wonder about the reliability of the information, and as a consequence, their knowledge is superficial. But in an era where the older generation complains about information overload, they show their shortcomings in dealing with information richness.

Information overload is typical for elder generations, *Homo zappiens* never complain about this phenomenon. In fact, having a multitude of resources available is a prerequisite for learning how to select and how to get to know what is reliable information or not. Of course, children may accept some information from the internet that in their parents' view is of no value, but would we like our children to select information using only verified information sources? Are we helping them by providing them with textbooks, daily newspapers or refereed journals? Although we might think that those information resources are trustful, we are not teaching them the skills to select and find trustful information.

In addition, we should recognize that newspapers, trusted newsreaders on television and textbooks do not always present objective and trustful information. History textbooks of almost any country are an example of how history can be distorted by national interests or local, cultural beliefs and values. Do we have to make up our minds about major political issues by watching only one television channel? One of the major benefits of technology has been that information is no longer a scarce commodity. It's available for almost anyone, anywhere in the world, and most important, at the same time.

That is why we should redefine the concept of information overload as information richness and embrace and celebrate it rather than complain about it. If children seem to act superficially with information found on the internet, we should realize that most of the time they collect information for homework. Since, for most children, homework is a pain because it's compulsory and therefore does not engage them, it's understandable why they're not very keen on determining the trustiness of the information found. Rather, they will look for whatever information is most easily found that meets the minimum criteria of satisfying the teacher. However, watch them working in a forum where they want to find a cheat code for playing Black & White, then they are very keen to get the right information, learning quickly how to distinguish who is to be trusted and who is not.

The issue of trustfulness of information is a long standing concern in information retrieval and production. In the past, libraries and scientific procedures of co-references have ensured that trusted bodies of knowledge developed and were shared among the community of interest. By contrast, information on the internet is chaotic and anyone can put anything on it. This situation was the case until similar procedures of certification came up through e-zines and new search engines, such as Google Scholar, were developed. The problem of trustworthiness of internet resources is a temporary issue and what will ultimately remain from the internet chaos is that our children have learned that information is abundant and that it comes from many different sources, even unreliable ones.

The major issue is not trustworthiness, but the skill of dealing with huge amounts of information and strategies on how to find the information you need most effectively and most efficiently. We must recognize that for future generations these skills cannot be trained in traditional libraries, we have to stimulate them to use digital sources for information retrieval. It's not likely that by the end of this century, information, whether scientifically oriented or not, will be available mainly through printed matter. We live in a disruptive age, where the analogous world is changing into a digital world. This demands new strategies for dealing with information and *Homo zappiens* appear to develop such strategies on the basis of how it comes to know information, colourful screens and interactive multimedia.

Multitasking

If you've been raised in the analogous age, your parents have probably taught you that doing one thing at a time guarantees success. I object to parents who still try to impose this rule on their children. Most children will reply with a kind smile and continue to do exactly the opposite. Listening to music is an important part of *Homo zappiens'* lifestyle. Most children do their homework while listening to their favourite music, using the playlist they have saved on their computer or MP3 player. And students in higher education walk around their faculties or work at computers while listening to their music files, using their iPods and MP3 players. It's common to meet students at a teacher training college multitasking while surfing the internet, listening to their music in one ear, and communicating with a peer student through the other. It's a very common phenomenon that can also be observed on public transport. Children are talking to each other, sending SMS to friends on their mobile phone, while all the time listening to their music through their MP3 player. And they do all this simultaneously. This is also true when *Homo zappiens* use MSN.

Microsoft[1] found that children communicate through MSN with ten children at a time and apparently enjoy it. When interviewing children on this behaviour, their answers reflect their skill at paying attention to various information sources simultaneously at different attention levels. They are able to increase or decrease their attention level for specific information sources, without muting one of them entirely and keeping a certain basic level for each of them. They immediately increase their attention to one information source as soon as they get some relevant cue, giving other information sources a lower level of attention, and decrease their attention as soon as they think it appropriate to switch to another source.

This way of dealing with information is much more intensive than listening to one source of information at a time. Former generations may think it exhausting, that multitasking cannot attain any quality, but *Homo zappiens* seem to have learned to exercise this strategy of raising and lowering their attention levels, switching from one to the other. *Homo zappiens* have gained experience which former generations have not. We should realize this when claiming that *Homo zappiens* are superficial. Aren't we projecting our own limitations of information processing skills on our children by saying that multitasking is worthless and even counter productive for knowledge acquisition? Or is our scepticism towards multitasking inspired by our firm belief

---

[1] From a PowerPoint presentation of Microsoft at an EPN Conference, The Hague, 2004.

that quality of work or learning can only be achieved by silently reading books and trying to interpret and remember the author's point of view?

Let's try to consider multitasking from another angle. Taking a positive point of view on the issue, we might defend the assumption that dealing with numerous information sources simultaneously is a valuable skill, should we find ourselves in the situation of having to deal with a large amount of information. In addition, we know that a lot of information in the future will be online and interactive. Multitasking then is a highly effective strategy to process various information channels at a time. This gives individuals the ability to process information, three or even four times faster. Processing more information, however, is just one part of the multitasking skill. The other and most important part of the multitasking skill is the capability to manage different attention levels simultaneously and recognize cues for increasing attention levels at the appropriate moment. By practising this skill of multitasking in playful situations, such as talking to friends and listening to their favourite music, we can see that by doing so, *Homo zappiens* acquire strategies of how to deal with multiple tasks.

You might question if this skill is that important for learning. It goes without saying that *Homo zappiens* will have jobs in which they will need this skill. As knowledge has become a crucial asset for our current economies and employees become lifelong learners at the workplace, we can no longer hold our ground that multitasking is the wrong strategy. Future employees will have to be able to respond to various inputs of information, oral requests, emails, phone calls, pop-up RSS feeds and other push technologies and information sources simultaneously. The success of their jobs will depend on their capacity to make decisions on a variety of simultaneous inputs where it's impossible to know everything. The art of knowledge workers in the future will be to make the right decision in situations of suboptimal knowledge of all aspects of the problem.

Multitasking is a skill that helps *Homo zappiens* to process various inputs of information and to value specific inputs as more important or relevant than others. As a consequence, multitasking is a critical skill for learning since it allows students to concentrate on what is important at any given time, by the ability to manage their multiple attention levels. If this reasoning makes sense, we can develop it even further. Imagine a child comes into a classroom where a teacher is the sole source of information. From the child's perspective, this classroom is an extremely poor information environment. There is just one information source to listen to and, in addition, this information source is obligatory. The child is not in control of the information flow, which as we have seen in Chapter 2 is an almost natural condition for *Homo zappiens*. Traditional classroom teaching severely restricts the number of information sources and tasks, and keeps children out of control of which information or task to choose from – a teaching method that is highly unnatural for *Homo zappiens* and, as a consequence, is counter productive for learning.

Zapping

Ever since the 1950s, watching television has become a common activity in Western living rooms. The introduction of this technology has been impressive but not without concern. There were some who thought it would destroy family life and have tremendous consequences for societal structures, making entire populations dumb by reducing the ability of critical thinking. And although some of these concerns have appeared to be well grounded, television screens have grown bigger, flatter, and the number of television channels has increased unabated. With an ordinary dish antenna, driven by a small motor, you can watch and listen to more than a thousand television channels and radio stations. Fortunately, most of these channels are not in your native language, which makes watching difficult for many of us. But the choice is almost unlimited and the possibility of watching Dubai or Morocco television provides opportunities of cultural anthropological observations without leaving your home.

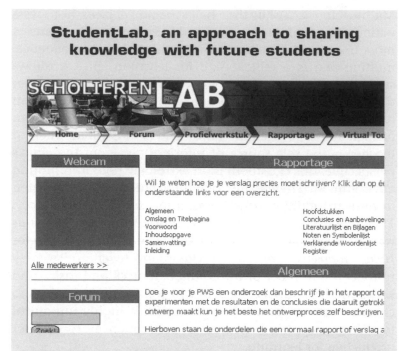

StudentLab, an approach to sharing knowledge with future students

StudentLab ('scholierenlab') is an online service provided by Delft University of Technology to help students in the last two grades of Dutch secondary education. These students are required to do a research project addressing a topic or issue related to their focal subject matter, such as sciences. StudentLab supports any secondary student looking for help in setting up research, defining relevant research questions, and answering focused questions requiring high levels of subject matter expertise.

Students may, while searching the internet, have a hard time finding the appropriate resources, or, should they find them, have a hard time understanding often academic level texts and information. As a means of providing expertise, StudentLab offers a portal for students in secondary education to reach the appropriate expert at Delft University of Technology. It's also an excellent means of sharing scientific research: whenever experiments are started that may be of interest to students researching their assignments, they are advertised on StudentLab. Students can then be brought into contact with the researchers for real-life visits and first-hand experience of the experiments themselves.

The StudentLab site is manned by five to ten students at Delft University of Technology, who monitor the forum and answer questions, as well as maintaining a list of links to online resources in various scientific disciplines. Resources and the forum are grouped according to the current grouping of classes in secondary education with topics such as biology, physics, chemistry, Earth sciences, management and organization, informatics, maths and general studies. Whenever the forum administrators are presented with questions for which they need more expertise, they find the appropriate professor to help them. Once they have the answer they need, they then take care of providing electronic feedback on the question, having learned themselves in the process.

In effect, this system is a cascaded form of mentor-pupil relations long distance, where the 'more educated' students at Delft University of Technology provide answers to their juniors in the highest levels of secondary education, with a little help from professors when needed. The system also helps raise the level of the assignments in secondary education, as those students using it are better able to deal with more complex subjects. Lastly, the StudentLab provides free promotion for Delft University of Technology as a place where knowledge is created and shared: a good place for students to go for their technical (Bachelors and) Masters after they've finished secondary school.

With such a choice of television channels, children today come to an understanding of information flows that differs profoundly from former generations. They have a 'free' choice of information and can, very similar to what they do when doing their homework, control various information channels at a time. Watching television for them is a particular way of multitasking. It's even more intriguing as they zap between television channels watching four or five channels simultaneously. It must be said, zapping is a very a-social activity, you cannot do it together. Having said this, zapping appears to be more than a strategy for avoiding boredom. Zapping channels requires good knowledge of more or less standardized formats or structures of audio-visual information flows.

Documentaries have different structures than films or soap operas. Each of these audio-visuals has specific formats that *Homo zappiens* appear to know better than former generations. *Homo zappiens* are able to recognize instances in films, documentaries and other television programmes that are less critical to know in order to understand the core of the message or flow of events. They've been watching television for so long that they've come to understand how film makers create their films and how documentary makers tell their stories. In particular, they understand that film makers communicate their messages through images – that the message is in the images. Parents mostly think it's in the text spoken by actors, explaining the message through conversations. But film is about visual communication and *Homo zappiens* understand this very well.

That is why they are able to zap from one channel to another at moments when they expect the film maker not to communicate important messages. It's by zapping that *Homo zappiens* are able to pick up bits and pieces of different information flows in a way that means they don't miss the important stuff. As a consequence, *Homo zappiens* are able to process discontinued information and give a concise summary of the various television programmes watched.

The main issue here is that zapping is the skill of determining essential kernels of information from an information flow and, on the basis of these kernels, constructing a meaningful whole of knowledge.

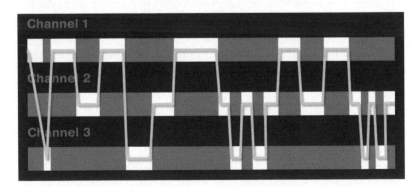

Figure 3.1 Channel zapping, absorbing discontinuous information

The zapping skill leads children to process three or more times more information in an hour than an adult. Their television watching behaviour is an active process of scanning for crucial cues and kernels rather than letting yourself go with the entire flow of events, conversations and image sequences. This skill has become that natural for them that they also apply it in their own communications in chat rooms and MSN environments. Even in their conversations they talk SMS or MSN language. You may have noticed that children can be impatient while listening to you answer their questions: *'Please, get to the point, you're talking too long.'* Homo zappiens think teachers are extremely slow in their explanations and in their answers to questions, willing to explain everything in detail.

You might think that *Homo zappiens* show an extremely superficial behaviour here. Is not the knowledge and expertise in the detail? This might well be, but *Homo zappiens* appear to think in structures of concepts and the interrelation between the concepts. This is what television has taught them to do and what has helped them in dealing with information overload. The major information processing activity in information rich environments is to look for conceptual structures first, getting the big picture, the overview. Details come later. In such circumstances, it is not being superficial not to focus on details, on the contrary, it's crucial not to focus on details in order to avoid getting lost in the information richness. Hence, focusing on details is an inappropriate strategy for dealing with information overload. We should realize here that *Homo zappiens* are not that different from former generations. Scanning newspapers by reading only the headlines is a well-known reading strategy in order to get an overview of the latest news, especially if time is restricted.

In fact, the zapping behaviour of *Homo zappiens* is not a new phenomenon in the sense that we have to use strategies to create order and rankings in information that is abundant. In addition to this, we may notice that many parents have adopted zapping strategies when watching television as well. However, we doubt if they're making similar decisions when zapping as *Homo zappiens*. Parents have never learned to extract information from images or video sequences, they have been trained in understanding texts mainly. That is why we presume that their zapping skills relate more to boredom about a television programme than searching to intensify information processing. In fact, processing three or more channels simultaneously demands an intensive action and implies more brainwork than when watching one television channel and letting yourself be immersed in just one programme.

Homo zappiens do not restrict themselves to passive television watching or at least not most of the time; children get bored when information is poor or comes in too slowly. If this point of view holds then it would also appear that children today want the answers to their questions quickly. They're used to intensive and multiple information processing activities. To them, your answer is just a single information flow, dealt with as if it was a piece of a television programme. *Homo zappiens* are searching for meaning, searching for the kernel, the message. Once it has picked that up it might zap you. You might well experience their way of information processing the other way around. By asking them a question, they will answer you the same way as they would like you to speak to them: short and to the point. You may also notice that you have to listen very carefully since every word seems to be of importance. No chance of relaxing, you have to concentrate!

Concluding, we might say that zapping television channels is the skill of processing discontinued audio-visual information flows and constructing a meaningful whole of knowledge out of it. As future information flows will progressively depend on audio-visual materials, this information processing skill seems to be crucial for future life and work.

Non-linear behaviour

When I was a child, I learned to read books from the beginning to the end. This became a natural skill that I continued to apply until I went to university. As the number of pages I had to read steadily increased, I had to unlearn my linear way of reading. Scanning texts was the major strategy I had to develop in order to keep control of the ever growing number of publications in my field of study. Nevertheless, texts were still the major source of information and the formats of these texts were highly linear: introduction, problem statement and research questions, methodology, data collection, data analysis, results and conclusions. Once you know the different formats for scientific books and articles, you can skip parts of the publication, choosing instead to go directly to the paragraphs of your interest. In fact, former generations of academics have developed strategies to deal with information overload in this way.

Homo zappiens have also developed strategies to do the same, but at a far earlier age than going to university, and with different and non-linear resources. Hence, strategies also differ in the sense that information is no longer exclusively analogue and in printed matter. Many information sources today are digital and/or multimedia. If information is digital and text only, it can be manipulated differently from printed matter. All of my students use 'CTRL-F' for searching scientific articles, their strategies focused on keywords. They can quickly search huge amounts of resources by using this approach and having selected relevant articles, they can analyse them using the same 'CTRL-F' command, using detailed keywords.

Students read only those paragraphs that seem most appropriate to them and those they are able to make sense out of from the bits and pieces of information. How can we best describe this skill? In fact, this skill consists of a number of sub-skills. The first one is that of defining a search question – what is my goal in searching these resources? How does it relate to what I have to deliver or achieve? This skill or even attitude is crucial. It relates to an active and critical learning approach. It helps students to avoid getting submerged by the author's argumentation and limiting learning to the level of understanding of what others have created.

Netvibes, your personal online window on the internet

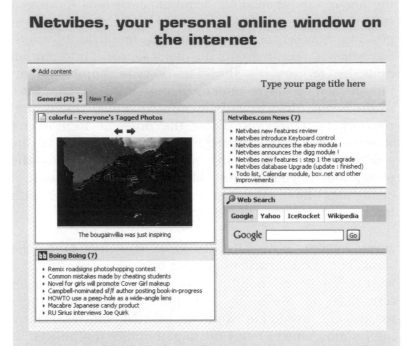

In essence, Netvibes is nothing more than a customizable portal, a site on the internet which provides links to your most important online resources, according to your own preferences. It can hold your favourite websites, but also provides functionality to view online multimedia without additionally required software. You can link into your email and other streams of information. Several of the large companies, such as Google, Yahoo and Microsoft, offer similar services. What makes Netvibes interesting is that it focuses primarily on 'web 2.0' and its applications.

The following extract is taken from an article by Tim O'Reilly (2005), who was part of the initial brainstorming that coined the term 'web 2.0' as a name for what the internet would become after the bubble burst in 2001. He claims that web 2.0 companies should incorporate some of the following traits, where more is better, but excellence in one area may be preferable to a little in all.

The web 2.0 philosophy aims at a paradigm shift in software development and online services. Where the web 1.0 age was characterized by the production of centrally developed, maintained and managed software packages, web 2.0 applications use open sources and provide much more control to the users. Users form networks of expertise in which each can contribute to the development of applications. Examples of such applications are Moodle, LAMS and Drupal. In addition, the focus is not on applications but on services. Wikipedia is a well known online service in which thousands of individuals contribute to a common and agreed body of knowledge.

Hence, the web 2.0 philosophy can be characterized as focusing on:

- services, not packaged software, with cost-effective scalability
- control over unique, hard-to-re-create data sources that get richer as more people use them
- trusting users as co-developers
- harnessing collective intelligence
- leveraging the long tail through customer self-service
- software above the level of a single device
- lightweight user interfaces, development models, and business models.

According to many, the internet is evolving from a controlled information repository to a community network, where information is still a commodity, but true value is in trust, acceptance, communication and collective intelligence. The tools described in boxes throughout this book all have various aspects of web 2.0, which was the main reason they were selected as examples. A full version of Tim O'Reilly's article on web 2.0 can be found at www.oreillynet.com/pub/a/oreilly/tim/news/2005/09/30/what-is-web-20.html.

Although the Netvibes initiative is still relatively new, it's interesting to note that they fully focus on bringing out the best that the internet has to offer, without primary concern for commercial interest. This is in line with the theory of network economies where the value lies in the use and the support by the network, that is, market share.

In addition to user control, Netvibes provides for new 'netizens', or citizens on the net, an online customizable portal that could function as a laptop. Instead of buying their own computer, they can time-share a machine with, say, a colleague and still be able to have their own configured settings and preferences.

Defining a clear learning goal is a prerequisite for learning at higher levels. Non-linear approaches are directed by enquiry of the learner and as digital information is accessible through strategies other than reading, non-linear approaches foster active learning strategies. The second sub-skill of non-linear learning approaches is the skill of determining the right keywords. It's striking to see that children are very competent in creating keywords that lead to success. They are so practised in the skill of searching information for specific goals that they've developed the ability of using a variety of keywords for finding information. If one keyword does not work, try three others.

The third sub-skill of non-linear approaches is the very same skill that children develop from watching television. They extract bits and pieces from various information channels to construct meaningful knowledge from all of these parts. As such, this sub-skill is also known from former generations who did the same with textual information trying to build new knowledge when writing new articles or books. However, *Homo zappiens* have learned this skill in real life, whereas the former generations did this within the framework of formal, mostly higher, education. The other difference is that *Homo zappiens* develop this skill not only with textual information but also multimedia resources, which have different formats than printed matter. The format of audio-visuals, such as documentaries or films, is quite different from texts. And children have come to understand how to interpret images as we saw earlier in the paragraph on iconic skills.

To conclude, we can see that *Homo zappiens* use specific skills to master information flows and learn through enquiry. The learner is at the centre of the learning process, he or she deciding what questions and sequences of questions will be defined and answered. As a consequence, *Homo zappiens* are active learners taking a non-linear approach in which they formulate the sequence of search questions to be addressed.

Collaborative skills

Playing computer games started as a stand alone activity in the 1980s. Since then, computer games have evolved into a community oriented activity. Many popular games, such as the World of Warcraft or Second Life, have extensive communities on the internet where players can not only communicate about the game but also buy and sell items placed on the notice board for instance. Although these community activities are a spin-off of the computer games as such, the games by themselves also contain many group activities. In the World of Warcraft these communities are called guilds – groups of individual players who work together to solve the quests or problems in the game. In fact, the game is a sequence of problems that becomes more complex as the player advances to higher levels. The more complex the problems become, the more players have to collaborate to solve them. An individual player is not able to achieve the highest level without organizing groups of players to solve problems collaboratively, sometimes with as many as up to 40 players or more at a time.

Collaboration is a common strategy within many computer games, even in games such as Counter Strike, which may seem violent to outsiders but which require team work to achieve goals. What children seem to learn from these games is that collaboration is a viable strategy to overcome and solve problems. They learn that competition is another strategy and it depends on the situation as to which strategy might be most effective. Collaboration also includes sub-skills, such as organization skills. If a gamer has to build a team of players to solve a problem, how do you organize such a team? What skills are required and how should these skills be combined to work together? Hence, collaboration demands leadership, planning and social skills. These social skills relate to norms and attitudes that develop during the game. For example, when involved in a quest in the World of Warcraft, you should not leave this activity before the problem is solved. If you do, it will be extremely difficult to organize a team of players in future since your reputation as someone who leaves his friends in a difficult situation will be widespread among the community, even beyond your guild.

Social skills are also involved as guilds have guild leaders who plan social activities. It is not unusual that guild members meet up in the game at a specific time and place to take a picture of themselves, or rather, their game characters representing the guild. Communication is often extended beyond the standard chat facility in the game by installing a VoIP (voice-over IP) tool, such as Teamspeak. Players can talk in real time to each other while playing the game, discussing the best strategies and keeping in close contact when going into dangerous dungeons. Guilds may consist of players from different countries, agreeing on a common communication language. As a consequence, children are accustomed to operating in international teams. If you're a fanatic player of a specific game that runs on the internet, your online friends might become far more important to you than your neighbours, at least within the world of this game.

Acting in virtual communities is nothing new to *Homo zappiens* and is part of normal life. Both real life and virtual life are components of their lives, without considering one less valuable or real than the other. How is learning concerned here then? As learning resources will mostly be online in the future, it's important to have the right skills to communicate with those who can help you to access them, discuss their meaning and to share your own knowledge with them. Here, the above mentioned social skills work perfectly well. Problem solving is also an important skill for learning and for life and will probably be a major skill for lifelong learners and knowledge workers. Having developed skills that help to define and categorize problems and to decide on the most appropriate strategy to employ, gives individuals major advantages in their learning and working environments.

We have tried here to make some connections between *Homo zappiens'* behaviour and learning by putting forward some major skills that children seem to develop using information and communication technology. There are other skills that have been defined by researchers, such as Gee, Goodson et al. and Turkle that are worthwhile to consider. But it's not our intention to be exhaustive. We want to make it clear that we should realize that using information and communication technology like children do can help our education to perform better. Digital thinkers, as our children are, can do a lot more than is traditionally expected from them in schools. We can challenge them by putting forward complex problems to solve and giving them extensive control of their learning process. They like to be challenged as they have experienced this from playing many computer games. They also like to be challenged with complex tasks. The traditional pedagogical approach of working step-by-step is not their thing. They are non-linear – it's more challenging. They like to be immersed in situations where you don't know where to start and how to act. They like experiential learning as many computer games are exactly that. What they don't like is a classroom where they have no control and where there's only one single information flow and nobody to collaborate, negotiate or communicate ('*mobile phones off!*') with. That is a situation far from their daily experiences at home when they are playing games and communicating in international teams.

In fact, *Homo zappiens* are challenging education to exploit their skills and strategies far more than it does now. Computer games can play an important role in new ways of exploring science and humanity alike. Computer games are engaging children in learning; a game immerses players in an itinerary of discovery which motivates them in a playful way. Immersion and motivation are critical aspects of deep learning. By intertwining play and learning, we can tap into children's fantasy, which itself is an important factor in fostering creativity. After all, weren't we supposed to develop a creative society? How can we do this if we let students only reproduce what others have found out? If education could succeed in combining play and learning, schools could become the meeting place to be for children who are so proficient in virtual environments.

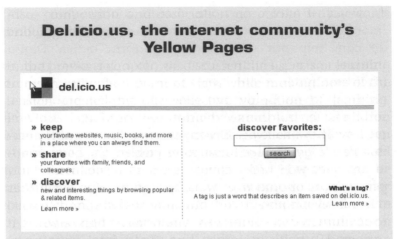

Del.icio.us, the internet community's Yellow Pages

del.icio.us

» **keep**
your favorite websites, music, books, and more in a place where you can always find them.

» **share**
your favorites with family, friends, and colleagues.

» **discover**
new and interesting things by browsing popular & related items.

Learn more »

discover favorites:

search

What's a tag?
A tag is just a word that describes an item saved on del.icio.us.
Learn more »

Del.icio.us can be described as a collaborative effort at indexing the internet. Any user may collect an online list of his or her personal favourite websites. You may then share this list with others and thus link into a network of lists. This way, a community filter on the internet is slowly growing, whereby on each topic, favourite sites are designated to provide the quickest path to certain information. Over the last decade, information overload has been a phrase often heard and Del.icio.us may just be a web 2.0 solution.

Maybe as little as ten years ago, people considered learning certain information by heart as the best way to improve your knowledge, skills or competences. If you wanted to be a good taxi driver or courier, this meant you needed to be able to get from point A to point B in the quickest possible time. Accordingly, you would memorize large chunks of maps, so you could go from London to Paris without the tedious searching through indices.

Nowadays, information is changing rapidly. The best road from A to B may change location each week, due to road repairs for instance. So it's the same with the internet. It has become impossible to stay up to date with all the new developments in technology. The moment you learn this information, it's already outdated. You will notice that *Homo zappiens* have developed an effective system to deal with this rapidly changing flow and value of information: they no longer memorize the information, simply the links to web pages and websites or other such locations on the internet, where they know they will be able to find the most accurate information at the time they need it.

Ask your son or daughter to tell you which mobile phone is best for you. They will not tell you, since a new mobile telephone device is produced almost daily. Instead they will give you the address of a website where all the various mobile phone models are compared; where a community is contributing to keeping the comparison accurate for the exact purpose you now require this information. Your youngster has effectively reduced the complexity of this huge network of information to one line of reference.

Combining this example of 'reference memory' with the ever growing need for 'any time, any place', Del.icio.us is developing as a collective hive for online reference memory. Apart from helping a community to reference the internet, Del.icio.us also provides you with your personal reference favourites, conveniently available to you wherever you go, should there be an internet connection and the need to use them.

Learning playfully

> **❝** *Treat people as if they were what they ought to be and you help them to become what they are capable of being.* **❞**

Johann Wolfgang von Goethe

In previous chapters, we have described a new generation of children growing up amidst information and communication technology; we described them as *digital thinkers* and have tried to give you their view on technology, which to them has always been there but to you may seem new, even revolutionary. We have tried to put a name to the most important, distinctive skills these children seem to be developing, which set them apart from us and makes us label them '*Homo zappiens*' – a new sort of human. Also, we touched upon the similarities between gaming and learning.

In this chapter, we will reflect on the learning aspects of *Homo zappiens'* behaviour. We will try to translate the skills that were described in Chapter 3 on our current view of society, to try and demonstrate further how they may be seen as useful in learning. The main question to answer in this chapter is if and how learning has changed because of technology. To do this, we must first take a closer look at learning itself – what it is and how it can be defined.

Man is, by nature, an inquisitive creature: we do not just accept and live with what is there; we seek new things, new opportunities and new ways to improve our lives. Maslow (1987) captured our motivation for behaviour in his layered pyramid model, trying to explain how we prioritize between living our lives and improving our lives. As we improve our lives, we use our brains as instruments to analyse and adapt to our surroundings and predict our uncertain future. This ability to recognize patterns in our experiences and improve our responses to them is what we call 'learning'. We use knowledge, skills and values to make up the competences that determine those responses.

We try to communicate our competences by information and examples so that others may profit from our discoveries and we, in turn, may profit from the growth of the whole. We call this phenomenon teaching, coaching, training, educating, drilling, conditioning, manipulating or leading, all dependent on the intentions we have for our communications and the ways this leads us to structure what we communicate.

One of the reasons for learning is that it allows us to optimize our response to a certain situation, so that we may minimize the risk of uncertainty and doubt. One of the reasons for interpersonal communication is that we, as a species, have recognized the benefits of distributing tasks and efforts: it's far easier to copy something from someone else than it would be to (re)invent the same thing. A further continuance of specialization can be seen in the invention of teaching: those individuals who are particularly skilled or knowledgeable on a certain subject are given the task of educating their successors, so that their particular abilities will not be lost. Over time, we have developed organizations for teaching and education to further increase the efficiency with which we guard valuable skills and knowledge for our species.

For this chapter, it's important to realize that there are certain aspects of learning that can (only) be done individually and aspects which require communication. The acquisition of information and the consequent transition into knowledge is based on what the individual thinks is important. However, one's personal values are strongly influenced by one's surroundings and the conventions that have been negotiated. Whenever groups of people have to coexist, they negotiate conventions and rules to regulate the impact of other people on their surroundings.

Skills are abilities of the individual, strongly connected to one's personal strengths, but the development and use of them is influenced by the requirements imposed on the individual by its surroundings.

The two pictures (figures 4.1 and 4.2 over the page) are an illustration of how technology has visibly impacted the lives of children. In the previous chapter, we discussed the increased prominence of television in society. You might say we have rediscovered the pleasure of communicating in images, akin to early cave drawings. Some of the most important objections parents seem to have to their children playing computer games is that they get too little physical exercise and social interaction. On the point of physical exercise we tend to agree, because technology has enabled us, in all aspects of our lives, to become lazy. Take the simple example of food again: we no longer need to hunt for food or grow it; we can have it delivered after a simple purchase over the telephone or on the internet.

The problem that our minds seem to be becoming the main, if not the only, important aspect of our being is growing because of the possibilities to express ourselves by other means than physically. This book, however, is not the place to discuss lengthy considerations on how our society is growing fat and (physically) unhealthy. We are exploring the possibilities for our minds and, indeed, to be more specific, the perceived changes in our children. That's how we come to the second point of children not having enough social interaction. In the previous chapter we showed you how, in fact, the interactions taking place in online gaming are very much social in nature and may even be more crucial for the future of *Homo zappiens* than playing outside

Figure 9.1 Children playing

Figure 9.2 Children playing cards online

Homo Zappiens: Growing up in a digital age

with neighbouring children. It's through the way we were brought up that we now look at the world. We relate how we should raise our children to how we were raised ourselves. So, if we were to look at *Homo zappiens* gaming and try to translate this into examples from our own youth, we might be able to better understand how indeed they might be learning. We shall try to demonstrate this with the following test.

Take the following example: a ten-year-old child comes home from school one day and after having a glass of lemonade and some snacks or fruit, it would normally be time for play. We will assume this child is either smart enough or diligent enough to have already finished its homework. Outside, rain is pouring heavily and if you yourself had nothing else to do, you could see yourself sitting by the fire gazing at either the flames or the pages of a book, smelling the fumes of fresh pinewood burning. Your favourite record is playing softly in the background. You could call the weather wintery and would not want to go outside yourself, as neither does the child. What would you have this child do?

A Propose to play a board game with you, such as Risk or Monopoly.

B Talk to you about experiences at school and ask about your school days.

C Read a book by Charles Dickens.

D Write an essay for the upcoming best school science idea contest.

Your child is experiencing difficulty with a child from the neighbourhood and is consistently being bullied on the way home from school. You think it's best if you stay out of the situation and let the child resolve the issue themself. In your opinion, how should your child react?

A Consider the bully may have a specific territory and try new routes.

B Alter posture and expression until it intuitively creates a stand-off.

C   Look at the bully's friends and copy their behaviour.

D   Discuss with you how to handle the situation and propose a plan.

Following these two example questions, it would be very interesting to know how you answered and what you think can be said about the results (don't peek ahead!). Also, we'd like to know if you have ideas for further questions which might be added to the next edition of this book. Please take a moment to share your thoughts with us at www.homozappiens.nl or send an email to: book@homozappiens.nl.

Good, now the final part of the test is complete. What we could do with these results is give you a small indication of your preference towards learning, since the questions were loosely based on Kolb's (1984) learning styles. We will explain this in the next chapter. We could also try to conclude whether you consider learning more successful if it produces results, involves interaction, is entertaining or increases knowledge. Obviously, by the choice of words the questions are slightly biased, since, for instance, we mentioned the word 'play' prior to the first question, which might have prompted you to answer 'A' more often.

The most important reason for writing the test you just read was to get you to use your brain as the tool it's intended to be: an active instrument of simulation. While we might conclude some things about how you are wired, we can with certainty say that we made you imagine, incited you to test yourself, got you involved and made the first part of this chapter interactive. Maybe you even considered it fun and refreshing.

Consider again the following: a child playing a computer game, which involves picking up weapons, blasting some monsters and scoring points for damsels-in-distress saved, is doing exactly the same thing you just did, just on another subject. It's imagining itself some place it is not, acting in a manner that it does not usually display (not to say that it might not want to) and making choices based on this virtual situation. It's challenging itself to rescue as many damsels

Skype, the future of person-to-person communication?

Technology is advancing and, at the same time, traditionally separated fields of application are merging and new applications emerging. For years we have seen the fields of information technology (IT), communication technology (CT) and multimedia growing together to form what is now considered as ICT. Computers lie close to the heart of the ICT applications sphere because of their many diverse uses and, as such, have driven most of the convergence but we have also seen mobile phones gaining markets, then cameras and internet access and, lately, merging with PDAs, personal digital assistants or small computers with basic organization and communication functionalities. The keywords seem to be connected, integrated and portable.

As a result of communication networks merging with the internet, the nature and protocols of network transmission have become more packet oriented. When many different connections need to be made between sources and demand, in rapid succession, with only little information bandwidth travelling between source and demand, it is uneconomical to dedicate a full connection between source and demand for the duration of the requirement and the bandwidth at its peak. Instead, the data sent can be split into small chunks (packets), each of which can be sent along the fastest route between A and B and reassembled at the point of arrival. This is the fundamental difference between circuit-switched and packet-switched networks, or for example, between traditional phone networks and the internet.

Voice-over IP (VoIP) is a means of sending, for instance, telephone conversations through a packet-network and Skype is a service that facilitates both the VoIP connection as well as, for a fee, the connection between the IP and circuit networks. The software allows you to telephone between two or more computers, which must be connected to the internet, for no extra cost than maintaining the internet connection. We see similar functionality in other major chat software, for instance, MSN, AOL or ICQ (I seek you). What is interesting, however, is that Skype will also allow you to connect your internet connected computer to someone's telephone at the cost of a local connection or to be reachable on a single number/account for a local fee in many countries around the globe. At the time of writing this, it costs a mere £0.01 per minute from the UK to a telephone landline in Italy using Skype.

Voice-over IP effectively lowers the barriers for less technically interested people to use the benefits of technology. In addition, as an added extra, it offers free video-telephony between computers enabled with cameras, making use of the ever increasing bandwidth of the internet. As more users upgrade to broadband connections, we will see the application of stand alone video-telephony sets emerge.

VoIP has one major disadvantage, which is currently still being worked on but is a core problem for all packet-switched networks: quality of service (QoS). As packets may travel from A to B through, for instance, either C, D or E, a stream of packets may have variable delay times according to network usage at the instance of transmission. This may create some stuttering in telephone conversations, or blur in video streams, and is really the only reason for sometimes maintaining a dedicated connection.

and kill as many monsters, just as you might have challenged yourself to predict our intentions for the test. Whenever it accurately predicts that a damsel will move to the right and it's therefore safe to fire a rocket directly at the monster behind the damsel, it feels joy the same way you might have felt good by contributing to our website community (see page 84 for contact details). Interestingly enough, how many of you have made this sort of comparison before? And how many of you readers agree that this comparison holds?

If we had given you this test in a traditional classroom setting, we would most certainly have witnessed peer pressure to answer the questions, more strategic behaviour, more response via email and on the website, and less enjoyment. We might have made the test more 'productive' in terms of feedback at the expense of personal freedom to choose to participate. In terms of the example of a child blasting monsters: if we had given it the game and then positioned ourselves directly behind the child, noticeably using a stopwatch and taking close note of the score, we would have increased the stress level and probably as much as half the children tested would have enjoyed the game less or performed less. Certainly they would have been more goal driven and thus would have taken less notice of the paintings on the walls of the game environment. They would have almost instantly noticed what our criteria for judging were and responded in kind by setting different goals, to stop us from breathing down their necks as quickly as possible.

Now, if it was your goal to have as many virtual monsters killed as possible, you might be happy with the result. However, was it not our intention to trigger certain behaviour, to offer an immersive virtual environment to practise certain skills of prediction and creative solution? There certainly is the opportunity for both and it will depend on you and your situation what goal you prefer. In the same measure, your own personal situation will determine how you prefer to learn certain skills, knowledge and values, but as we've said before, this situation is not only influenced by your own personal strengths but also by the information you can acquire and the values you have negotiated. The main thing to consider here is that motivation for learning is personal: how you do it, when you do it, where you do it, why you do it and even whether you do it. As soon as we start restricting you, we may get you to learn a particular thing better, faster and with less effort on your part, but it will feel less as something you did to enhance yourself and more like an obligatory task that had to be completed to get someone to stop breathing down your neck. At the same time, we may have even stopped you from learning something else, which you considered more important. There is a natural tension between the needs of the individual and the needs of the collective, which leads us to compete with each other while at the same time needing one another. Sharp readers will have noticed a bit of critique on traditional schooling, but if you are looking for our opinion on current education, you will have to wait for (or skip ahead to) the next chapters.

Let us briefly summarize what has been said so far. We all learn. We learn by recognizing patterns in our experiences. We respond to our surroundings and this includes other human beings. The competences we use to respond to our environment consist of our knowledge, values and skills. While we learn skills that fit our personal strengths and we create knowledge from information that we, as individuals, find important and meaningful, the use of our skills and what we think is important, that is, our values, are based on our interaction with our surroundings.

Motivation for acting is based not only on personal, but also collective, goals. As a species, we have recognized the potential value of the individual and thereby the value of task specialization. This creates tension between the group and the individual: you must contribute on your own, but at the same time, you are dependent on others. The same tension exists for education (to be discussed in the next chapter): we need the individual to acquire the most important skills and knowledge that our species needs to preserve, but at the same time, we need the individual to develop its own strengths and contribute innovation (or stability).

To develop the personal competences necessary, we use our brains as a tool for simulation. We add our experiences, create abstract or alternate realities and develop and test our solutions to certain problems. When, inevitably, we encounter unpredicted situations, having simulated various similar scenarios allows us to choose the best match and thereby reduce the complexity and novelty of finding a solution. To clarify, consider the following examples:

1. As a child you have had history lessons. You know about the Second World War. This knowledge allows you to understand why other people react with fear or anger towards certain situations. It enables you to value the worth and contributions of others.

2. You have learned to play cards. Card games involve a measure of chance and are restricted by a discrete number. With sufficient skill it is possible to calculate the progress of the game. With sufficient skill it is also possible to mislead others regarding the probability of the game situation. These skills are useful when seeking to optimize self-centred gains.

3. Through discussion with others and because of the availability of so much information on the internet, you have learned to value information filtering skills in yourself and others. This drives you to develop your own skills and seek co-operation with those individuals who have more skill.

Over the last few pages, we have looked at learning, communication and individuals from the perspective of our species. We will now go back to looking through the eyes of the individual; the *Homo zappiens*. The reason for this quite lengthy introduction was to show you some notions that have always determined learning; notions that still determine learning. We can safely conclude that learning, in that respect, hasn't changed. Then why is it that we feel so much has changed? What change do we see? Before we gave you a test and discussed simulation and motivation, we mentioned social interaction: we have noticed our children committing less to physical social interaction. Instinctively, we feel that this is wrong, because we experienced a lot of benefit from similar social interaction in our youth.

We do not yet believe in the potential for new technology to substitute real physical interaction, mostly because we expect to be able to see and hear people and observe body language. These are our negotiated conventions for communication. Objectively speaking, we are partially right, in that technology still cannot fully substitute the 'look and feel' of physical get-togethers. At the same time, while we adjust our own conventions to fit in with this new technology, the new generation of children have negotiated their own set of conventions.

To *Homo zappiens*, it's perfectly agreeable to use every medium of communication available. They expect each other to value email and telephone communication in equal measure as physical contact. Consequently, they have no problem meeting each other and responding to an email they read the day before. They seem to lack the mistrust of technology that still prompts us to demand agreements and binding contracts in writing. Even though digital identity allows even more room for fraud than telephone and email, *Homo zappiens* have negotiated to accept this uncertainty so they can continue to reap the benefits of the technology. At the same time, they are developing skills to detect fraud, for instance, by noticing that one's style of writing on MSN is not the normal style or that shared knowledge suddenly seems to be lacking.

Technological development has increased the possibilities for *Homo zappiens* to learn. There is more information available from which to create knowledge. There are more media available to communicate competences and negotiate values. There are new forms of virtual environments that allow for better support in simulation and play. How petty must we seem to *Homo zappiens*, that we merely had clothes to dress up in and pretend to be a cowboy or an Indian? Nowadays, they have virtual avatars, computer alternated audible speech, and potentially even electric shocks to indicate they've been hit by an arrow or bullet. While sitting in their chairs behind a computer, they have a far more immersive and engaging virtual environment to simulate – exactly the same things we did.

Wikis and blogs are an interesting phenomenon. They read like books and traditional encyclopedias. While at the same time serving the purpose of information storage, they also allow manipulation and adaptation. With wikis we have created a knowledge tool that can be just as responsive to change as we are. Blogs make storytelling what it has always been when reading to small children: it allows room for questions.

The strength of the human mind, and according to Charles Darwin this quality should be attributed to living species in general, is its ability to adapt to a change in circumstances. We call this learning. What sets us apart from previous species, if indeed we may speak of evolution and we consider ourselves to be the latest specimen of our line, is that we have a stronger developed ability to project. We are capable of imagining ourselves outside physically perceived reality, not just in place and time but in ability and appearance as well. We say perceived reality because when we claim to be capable of virtualizing anything in our minds, how can we be certain of what we consider real? We will leave that line of thought for the philosophers.

When we play computer games or participate in simulation, we are pretending to know our environment. We may even be pretending to control our environment or have altered some aspects of ourselves or our surroundings. Children playing cowboys and Indians are conducting the same type of simulation as children playing World of Warcraft are, with the added benefit that the online game is much more immersive and flexible, allowing for a quick change of character without the hassle of changing costumes.

A human mind, capable of imagination, capable of adaptive behaviour, is a very powerful instrument. From birth we start to try to condition this instrument, as our species has done with rocks, metals, structures, chemicals and, most recently, atoms and electrons. This conditioning is done on multiple levels: we mould our minds to what is useful to ourselves as individuals, but also to the needs of our families, communities, societies, nations and species. And this is where a conflict of interest may exist: between the multiple levels of human interaction that try to mould our minds.

Every once in a while there is a collective awareness and reasoning that pushes all individuals in one direction. We can call this nature or a higher consciousness but every one of us will be able to find traces of this in our history: a natural disaster, the discovery of a technology, a strong leader or the birth of an ideal. These things have tremendous impact on how and what the individual does, because they change our environment; we change our perception of the environment.

That environment includes other individuals, for whichever way we look at it we are not truly individuals: we need each other. If you were truly acting on your own interest, say, for instance, you were isolated on another planet, you would not be reading a book, you would be growing crops (or given a certain level of intelligence and time, you would be managing a park of robots to grow crops for you). Books are stories told, captured in print: knowledge transferred from one entity to another in a certain form. Books are communication and you cannot communicate with yourself, with the exception of diaries that may be seen as artificially added memory.

As a species, we acknowledge our mind as a tool and we seek to use that tool to its fullest potential. We are still improving. One of the outcomes of developing this tool is that we created language: spoken symbols with which to communicate information in our quest to transfer knowledge. We accepted certain standards (for instance, language instead of images) and implemented valued rules as the basis for our communication. At least, the dominant part of our species did. Because of these constructs, we have enabled ourselves to absorb and digest much more information than we could have if we had stayed isolated individuals. Nature gave us the notion that we are better off together, but at the same time, stimulated individualism as a means for innovation. Look at large multinationals today: they are wealthy, continuous and established, but whenever they seek innovation they promote or acquire small start-up companies because these small units have the flexibility and adaptability to move fast, to think fast.

Governments operate on several levels, for different scales of problems. The distribution of housing and food to the needy is best taken care of at a local level, while the development of transmission technology for everyone is aggregated to a national and even international level. With a bit of cynicism, one might say that the larger the organization the less likely it is to be responsive to change. This has been captured in notions such as Newton's laws of physics, as well as modern repulsion for bureaucracies. We do, however, need collective structures and are constantly trying to attain collective consciousness and co-operation. Analysing modern democracies and autocracies, we can conclude that we have still not found a stable balance between individual and collective. Maybe we never will.

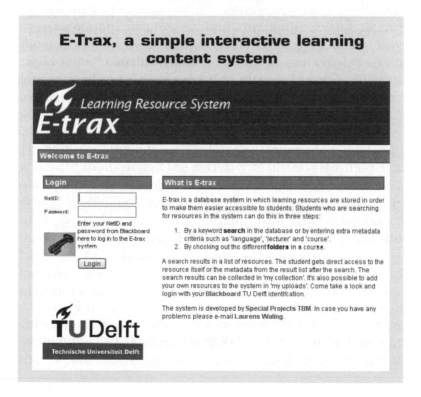

Teachers are using online resources more and more in their courses. Examples are papers, articles, books and readers put online, links to web pages or fragments of video or audio recordings. With little to no in-depth knowledge of the content management system and just barely the know-how to manage a single course, sharing resources between courses can be a pain in the rear, let alone having students submit their essays and such electronically through the system.

In an effort to support teachers in creating a more interactive, natural environment for future courses, E-trax was designed. This is a software system developed at Delft University of Technology, which aims to provide a more dynamic, interaction centred resource repository for courses. It basically can be added to any content system to make large repositories of content more manageable and useable.

E-trax was designed with the contribution of the community in mind, so both students and teachers would have the same interface. It allows you to upload your files to the system and label the file with appropriate keywords, title, author, and so on. It allows you to search the database on any of the fields of information a file can contain and provides you with a list of all matches. A ranking of the display is still being worked on. One of the advantages of displaying the results list is that it immediately allows you to identify whether a piece of information is an article, a sound clip, a video fragment, a web link or any of the other possible media types. When you've found resources of interest, the system allows you to tag those resources, so they are automatically remembered in your favourites list; should you ever need them again, or have to reference them repeatedly during a project, you will not have to search for them again.

The system also has a user rating tool, to rate a piece of content from zero to five stars. Any user can add his or her rating, without discrimination or weighting. This makes it an excellent tool, for instance, when jointly working on a project or peer reviewing essays and issue papers. As users rate the resources they find most valuable higher, one can decide to remove or archive low rated resources after a few cycles of use. It will also be easier for other users to quickly find the answers they need, as they'll be looking for five star resources first.

The second purpose of peer review in courses can be grading. Students could upload their papers into the system, after which everyone may read them and quote them as they like (much like scientific articles). A teacher could decide to make it mandatory that everyone rate, say, five to ten articles, assessing the relative value of each contribution by applying grades. This would of course leave room for fraud, but as with any community effort, trust is always a major component.

By handling content pieces as resources that may be labelled, searched, remembered and rated, the E-trax system is not only a search engine for local or external resources, it's also a community tool for managing those resources. It also acts as a teachers' aid in creating a more dynamic course environment on top of often control centred content management systems, which are heavily used today.

Now, back to our simple matter at hand, something as mundane as the learning individual. We mentioned change, adaptation, knowledge, skills, values, rules and conventions. We discussed individual and collective on multiple levels. This chapter detailed the mind as an instrument of virtualization to play with reality. In society, we saw a large swing of the pendulum towards mass standardization. Today, with the rise of pervasive information technology, we have enabled this pendulum to swing back. we are even going to see growing individuality and specialization, before again the pendulum will start moving towards its equilibrium. Why? Because we have started developing a more powerful communication tool than language. We are, in fact, rediscovering the potential of imagery, while at the same time upgrading our communication bandwidth to near brain speed. We know the developments our species went through, but who can say where it will lead us. Who can say or not if telepathy is waiting around the corner?

Any which way, the increase in communication potential has created room for the individual to assert a niche all of its own. With the creation of technology, we have shifted the balance between individual and collective towards the individual and therefore created more potential for change and innovation. As we labelled the era of mass standardization the 'Industrial Age', we will call this era the 'Creative Age'.

For the individual, these are turbulent times. We have gathered so much information and knowledge throughout the ages, and are able to communicate this so fast, that in order for an individual to serve a purpose in society, one has to start developing one's own potential in the womb. Keywords are self-understanding, self-control and self-expression. The first two are obvious: you need to know yourself and your key potential to be able to develop it, while at the same time you need to be in control of this development since you are the only one who has some inkling of where you're heading. Self-expression is, however, equally important and it pertains to maintaining the balance between individual and collective: we need each other and so we need communication. We must, therefore, acquire the skills of expressing our added value to our peers as we must learn to recognize the added value of our peers. Ten years ago, we attributed the same value to a career, loyalty and education; qualities that serve the masses first and then the individual.

Homo zappiens are growing up surrounded by technology. At the same time, these children are feeling the swing of the pendulum towards individual specialization and thus the need to be in control of their own development. The learning theory of constructivism asserts that children are most definitely not stupid; and certainly not empty vessels waiting to be filled by expert teachers. We have known this fact for a few decades but the full implication of this knowledge has only recently hit us in the face.

Homo zappiens, ever more so than previous generations, have taken control of their own destiny. Not because previous generations did not feel the same tug of the pendulum starting, but rather because they have finally been given the tools (technology) to do so. We perceive their behaviour and learning as radically different when contrasted to our own behaviour at that age, but we forget to see that this change is occurring on every level and age group in society; we forgot to see how very similar some activities are and how lucky *Homo zappiens* are to have the extra technology to broaden their minds.

Finally, to close this chapter and begin the next, we could say that there is a new sort of learning. Indeed there is. We have also just argued that a lot of what we think of as new is merely old processes taking place with new tools. There are, however, some things that have definitely changed and if there is one thing you should remember from reading this chapter, it would be that people in today's world require the freedom to accept uncertainty. Only those who can learn to live their potential, accepting that they cannot predict and control everything, will feel truly at home in the age of today and tomorrow. Then again, was this not always a part of growing up?

chapter 5

Stopping the roller coaster

It is, in fact, nothing short of a miracle that the modern methods of instruction have not yet entirely strangled the holy curiosity of enquiry.

Albert Einstein

People always learn. Even when you think they are committing the most useless activities imaginable, one could still say they are learning to be more experienced at doing something extremely useless. This gathering of experience is, generally speaking, not what we call learning though. We think of learning as some measurable or noticeable change in response to a certain situation. This very definition precludes the possibility of learning from a unique situation, since we will never have the opportunity of witnessing changed response to a situation that will not occur again. Now, obviously you're thinking: '*Wait a minute! That's not right,*' and of course, again, you are correct. Learning is no binary state in our perception, something you can either do or not do; there are various degrees of learning, at least to the observer, while a scientist may argue that learning is a binary activity.

Also, comparison and association go a long way towards bridging differences.

In the previous chapter, we discussed the aspects of learning from an individual point of view, while making note of the tension created by our collective valuation of learning. Previous chapters contained examples of children committing to all sorts of activities, which we have been conditioned to consider as not useful to learning. We showed you a breakdown of these activities and how they can be considered as learning. In fact, we saw that, so far, there has been a change in learning, and that this change is related to the tools and technology available for virtualization (simulation and play) and communication. There is a difference in what this new generation of *Homo zappiens* learns, because we have come to change our demands as a society, also because of our increased technology.

Lastly, there seems to be a shift in motivation for learning: because we've created room for the individual to specialize and contribute more to the collective, we're seeing more individuals using their self-consciousness, self-control and self-expression to determine their own learning goals. They're choosing their own ways of being facilitated, which, unfortunately, leads to a growing resentment of traditional education and schools as archaic institutions. In this chapter, we will take a look at these traditional manifestations of training and education. What do they offer and how does this fit with the seemingly changed demands of the *Homo zappiens*?

What can currently be seen in education is a struggle; a struggle to fit new technology into an old framework; a struggle even to serve society's changed demands with the existing framework. And it's failing. Not to say there are not plenty of examples of successful implementation of ELEs (electronic learning environments) or CBT (computer-based training). Most certainly there are many examples of teachers still delivering very interesting classes to their students. And most schools now have some way of coping with the pervasiveness of the internet and wealth of online information resources by having their students get their information from the internet instead of the local or school library. It's probably even true that every school now contains one or more computers. However, this is all too little, too slow.

Remember the emergence of colour television? Or more recently, the internet; let us discuss that. By some form of ingenuity we manage to develop new technology that actually enables us to do some very fun things: we can send email! Yes, that's right: the first use of the very early beginnings of the internet was networked communication. Then what did we do? We discovered we could use it to replace all sorts of existing technology and so the internet became the online library and data repository of the world, or to some cynics, a pornographic video store. In the process, we simply forgot that the added value of the network was actually its communicational capacity. Sure, we kept email; but we didn't build on the strengths of the internet; rather we took our precious time to reason out the full potential, while gradually using our new found technology to increase the efficiency of existing applications.

In the mean time, anything and anyone that didn't have an alternative, beat us to the punch and found a voice on the internet: the aforementioned pornography which found its anonymity, but also groups sharing illegal distributions of software, music, film, as well as oppressed minorities and even so-called terrorists. An early circulation, probably by means of a joke, was a document called 'The Terrorist's Cookbook'. In general, we saw the darker, oppressed side of society leading the development of an internet community.

In education, we see the same thing happening. The larger part of the educational system is still holding onto traditional values. It's a good thing it is, because if we stopped too suddenly and changed, we would have a very large mess to clean up. Society is not built to handle large, sudden changes as surely as large mass must take a large force to change its speed vector. And too bad that it is because if it started changing now, we might actually change along with society. For even though most people still don't use the full potential of the internet, the mere existence of those who can, our youngest generation, is driving up demand.

In the previous chapter, we discussed how people are taking more and more control over their own lives and learning, and how we see this most in our youngest generation. We gave you the story of the *Homo zappiens*, merrily gaming, chatting, zapping and multitasking its way through the virtual online jungles that society pretty soon will be calling 'home'. We explained how *Homo zappiens* are actually learning very critical skills for their future contributions to society, while all we see them doing are unclassified, unrated and thus useless activities. We can choose to see this phenomenon of actively pursuing the skills needed to become a modern, digital, creative, problem solver as something temporary or the start of a big change. If it's temporary, we can indeed continue the way we set things up. But what if this is just the beginning? Can we afford to neglect it?

We're used to knowing what is best for our children. We have to protect them from the big bad world that is life, at least until we are as certain as we possibly can be that they're able to handle themselves as we do. This means we want them to display the same traits that we ourselves display; we want to recognize those traits and abilities. So we tell them what to do, we check if they do this right and correct them if necessary. Quite a fun and useful approach actually – if we were cloning ourselves. We see puberty as a necessary evil, where our children learn to distinguish their own abilities. Rather, we would have them rebel less and just accept our knowledge and judgement. How often does the realization that parents actually meant best and were right come at around the age of 30?

It was for the good of us that our parents and teachers tried to teach us all there was to know. If we had not been put in contact with many different examples, if we had not experienced maths, sciences, languages, sports, music, culture, social behaviour, and so on, we would never have been able to develop the framework we now use to deal with the world around us. The only question we could raise would be: what if I had been able to experience more? Given that we might be able to experience only so many things in the 18 years we consider childhood, a better question would perhaps be: what if I had been able to select more interesting experiences?

The most important reason why humans developed as they did is because they worked together and shared their discoveries. From person to person and from generation to generation, the most useful tools, skills and knowledge have been passed on and, in the process, we developed the values and conventions to ensure the most efficient implementations. However, were those discoveries not made by headstrong individuals who were determined to try out something that was previously unknown or unheard of? We call them lucky accidents, the discovery of penicillin or the invention of the wheel. Someone just happened to stumble upon a discovery and managed to recognize its value. These individuals had one thing in common though: they were all inquisitive minds, who not only observed what was known, but looked for the unknown, the obviously missing; they were not afraid to try, not afraid to fail. Perhaps they even had an inborn sense or knowing and were actively seeking to acknowledge it. Certainly, these individuals were unrestricted by the morals and theories of their time. They were not hindered by the knowledge that something had not been possible until then. Instead, they had a youthful view of the world as if discovering it anew.

There were times when society considered young children as adults simply not fully grown, and treated them accordingly. They were of value immediately and were expected to act in such a manner. Then we 'discovered' that it was far better to protect children and let them play; to give them a time in their lives to experiment with who they are, what they could be and how they could and wanted to develop themselves. We gave them our framework of the world that they would be growing into and called this the educational system, which brought them discipline, information and accepted values to complement their experimenting and playful lives. This was a little over 100 years ago.

Over time, we have come to value dedicated, specialized workers with a specific task description, like the machines we employed to replace people whenever we could. We standardized our education to provide us with the best trained men and women for the job. We pumped people full of all the knowledge and skills that they would need to perform their tasks. We created structures, responsibilities, standards wherever we could and it seemed, for a time, that management science was the most important science everywhere we looked. Look at science today: researchers are burdened with a quota of publications to produce. What we did was re-frame and improve our framework until it was, in our opinion, the best framework possible for a child to use. While doing so, we had a specific purpose in mind: making children into productive adults. We created a mould that would fit only few and shape the rest. We forgot that the reason we gave them frameworks in the first place was to provide them with a safe environment for experimentation. For a time, the benefits outweighed the negative effects.

We have for some time been studying ourselves and how we could influence our conditioning. The science of behaviourism taught us that any skill or ability can be learned with sufficient stimulation (reward or penalty) and repetition. The theory was limited in that it considered human beings as black boxes, where you conditioned output by input and the process was irrelevant. To allow for a better understanding of what went on in the human mind, the theory of cognitivism was adopted. This theory views the mind much like a modern computer, where knowledge is stored, processed and linked to create an associative mental map of the world surrounding the individual. The theory suggests that if we pour enough information into an individual, it will become omniscient.

Currently, we have expanded on this view with the theory of constructivism, which presumes a more active role for the individual in the learning process. We can activate an individual by providing him/her with information, but we must also provide room for the individual to experiment with this information in order to create meaningful knowledge out of it. Social constructivism elaborated on the theory of constructivism stressing the interaction between peer learners as a critical component in the learning process. As a result, we now believe that knowledge resides in the negotiation of meaning between individuals. Most recently, George Siemens (2004) introduced the concept of connectivism, a first and most challenging attempt for a new learning theory, focusing on the role of information and communication technologies for learning. In his view, learning takes place primarily in a network of connected individuals, where knowledge also resides in the network itself and rests in diversity of opinions.

The influence of technologies is significant, as Siemens (2004) says, 'many of the processes previously handled by learning theories (especially in cognitive information processing) can now be offloaded to, or supported by, technology'. Tools (such as those examples in boxed text throughout this book) that *Homo zappiens* use for learning redefine and reshape our thinking. As a consequence, our learning behaviour is changing. Crucial learning activities are connecting a multitude of nodes of information sources, both human and non-human. Connectivism is an upcoming learning theory trying to incorporate the consequences of ever accelerating paces of information acquisition and changing knowledge through technologies.

Before information and communication technology appeared in our schools, David Kolb developed a theory that explains, in part, why a standardized approach to lectures or project based learning does not seem to work for all individuals. We touched on this theory in the previous chapter and shall explain it briefly here. An individual must go through various steps in his mind before something is learned. These four steps are:

- Observing concrete experience
- Reflection
- Forming abstract concepts
- Testing of concepts in new (related) situations.

Kolb suggests that at a certain point in its life, an individual will have a personal preference for focusing on a particular part of this cycle. This leads him to define four types of learning personalities and four types of behaviour. The theory is in agreement with constructivism, but expands on it by showing a growing need for individualization. A school that would base its education on Kolb's theory would offer a laboratory, a storytelling (aka lecturing) teacher, a lounge and a discussion forum to its students, allowing them to decide when, what and how much to use. We see similar designs in non-linear learning theory and non-linear design of technology based training.

Looking at the learning individual as someone who can be, act and respond differently from his or her peers, raises some very interesting questions regarding the structuring of current education. For instance, if we go through the four-stage cycle, does that imply that lectures are effective for only 25 per cent of our students? How does communication fit into the learning cycle and are there possibly issues that must be learned alone? And while we are still pondering those questions, once we know an individual's preference, can we rely that this will remain so forever? Or predict its response and development for the future?

Interestingly enough, if we look back at the developments in the way we think about learning and teaching, we see a trend towards the individual and towards self-motivation. The previous chapter saw us describe *Homo zappiens* as an entrepreneurial learner; one who takes his own view on the world and uses his own resources (which, by the way, often include teachers and experts) to solve a problem. In this chapter, we 'blamed' progress on individual risk takers, entrepreneurs if you will. With the development of technology, we have created room for the individual to contribute more. Logically, we will be discussing new methods of training the entrepreneur in the next chapter. The remainder of this chapter will be dedicated to showing you why.

Now, without wanting to push every school, college, university and training centre into the same corner, we will state that most learning institutions today are still working with a constructivist's view on education. You might remember that this theory suggests that time, activity and input are the three major variables that determine our level of learning and so the more senior are logically the experts or teachers. These experts have knowledge that can be put to a lot of good uses in organizations and the community, and so our system is designed to require as few as possible experts to educate all young individuals who want or need to learn. To enable this system to work, we have designed it around standards of tracking, control and stimulation.

New technology brought us change. We can suddenly access a lot of information and most of it much faster than we used to. These last few years have also seen us using the internet more and more as the added benefit it was from the start: a communication medium. Since computer technology has invaded all parts of our lives, it was only logical that it would not skip over one of the central institutions with which we are all confronted in our early youth: schools. Developed in parallel for corporate and school environments, we've seen a true explosion of electronic learning environments (ELEs), learning management systems (LMS), content management systems (CMS) and even learning content management systems (LCMS). These systems all have two aspects in common: they are meant to capture information exchange processes onto one platform and to support production of distribution frameworks. More simply put, these systems are meant to capture information and facilitate its productive use, for instance, in courses. They fit very well into our educational systems and thus met with a broad client base.

Many educational institutions have now implemented commercial learning management systems based on managerial rather than educational principles. Within the last five years we can see a paradigm shift in developing open source applications based on collaboration and sharing rather than on planning and control. With extensive investments in very reliable learning management systems, schools and universities face a next dilemma: continue to invest in ready to use and centrally developed systems that are hard to customize to institutional needs or invest in human capital for in-house customization of new software tools and platforms for learning.

Homo zappiens would definitely make a choice for the latter. The new generation of learners use the newest and most available in beta or gamma versions. They adopt easily new applications helping to do old things more efficiently, but mainly for reasons of being able to do new things not previously possible before. They prefer to learn in environments that coincide with their ways of communicating, uploading and sharing information. *Homo zappiens* are early adopters of new tools and platforms, applying their approaches learned in childhood. *Homo zappiens* see technology as a friend and consider all the possibilities of its doing both old and new things. This is why new tools and applications, such as social software, are rapidly spreading across the world; new generations of users understanding the meaning of new ways of communication, sharing and collaboration.

Something else entirely, which is rather funny if you think about it. We have embedded the concept of behavioural stimulus into our education. Stimulus leaving the possibility for reward and punishment. Yet we expect individuals to experience reward as a natural part of participating in the system and so most of our focus is on punishing deviant behaviour. We encourage children to be on time for classes, but we punish those who are late with extra 'quality time'. We expect students to develop their own potential for problem solving and then punish copying from others. We offer employees the opportunity to develop themselves and then oblige them to participate. We seem to have set up rather negative feedback.

Also, while we frown upon students copying from one another, we value research papers that quote from other established works. While we expect students to follow rules and examples, to adhere to discipline, we reward those employees who offer innovation with careers, higher salaries and more freedom. The feedback we provide in education does not seem to reflect what we expect from individuals in society. Small wonder that some *Homo zappiens* have already stated that school seems to be a place 'where you learn everything that you don't need in the real world'.

Let us think back on the situation we described: how education was once a complement to the playful and experimenting life of children. Should we want to return to a situation where young children are treated as adults and expected to contribute to society? Should we continue to protect children from the world around us, only to make the confrontation more abrupt once they turn 18, 20, 22 or whatever age they move out, get a job and start building their own lives? Or should we focus on letting children experiment and play and challenge them to contribute to what seems most appropriate and in line with their talents and passion? Such a discussion on education goes far beyond the very process of acquiring knowledge by individuals and groups of individuals. New technologies for learning are currently inciting such discussions as the uses of information and communication technologies hit the fundamentals of our concepts of learning and schooling. As learning is becoming a lifelong activity, we can no longer prepare children for a certificate that guarantees a job for life. The half-time value of knowledge is continuously shrinking and so our learning objectives should change accordingly. Know-what is no longer the most important goal, know-how, know-why and know-where are becoming the more required competences. If *Homo zappiens* are already preparing for future life, acquiring specific skills and competences, what could schools do to facilitate them to perform even better?

Someone once said that humans have only one truly original idea in their entire life. By its very definition this implies that the rest of the time what we do is copy. Copying is what we do to continue our existence as a species; we might also call this the transferral of knowledge and skills. If an individual's goal in life is to find that one truly unique thing that it can contribute to the collective, should then not the rest of his or her life be centred around learning to find and use its potential; discovering those skills, knowledge and values that will ultimately enable the creation of this idea? If we agree that the creative process exceeds the copying process in importance, that the individual and what it may produce is more important than what the collective may impart, that discovery and learning are the important activities and education is facilitating, why are we trying to stop the roller coaster of progress?

What schools could do

> The illiterate of the 21st century will not be those who cannot read and write, but those who cannot learn, unlearn, and relearn.
>
> Alvin Toffler

For five chapters we have been teasing you with ideas; some you may have known and others you may have recognized. We have highlighted some trends that may have brought forth *Homo zappiens* and we have shown some of the challenges that society is yet to face in fully accepting *Homo zappiens*. We promised you an opportunity to reflect on the role of education and learning in today's society. In this final chapter, we will tie together some of the concepts we have touched upon with the challenges facing us: we will give you our view of the necessary changes in our education systems and thinking to accommodate *Homo zappiens*.

Before we continue, let us once again state that it's not our intention to impose our ideas upon you. We wish for you to see opportunities for improvement in your learning and education, as well as that of your children, pupils or students. If, after reading, you still have doubts or counter arguments to our view and solution, please do not simply ignore them: share them with us. We realize that the current systems of education came to be for a reason and that they have served us well when we needed mass education for a society focused on production. In this book, we have given you a view on the changes confronting us. If you do not believe change is necessary, please do not spend more time considering it. On the other hand, if you think we should change something, please do not be discouraged if our suggestions lack a perfect match with your vision. As a last note, we would again like to point you to our website (www.homozappiens.nl), that will serve as a platform and opportunity for discussion on the topics of learning, education and technological progress.

Scenarios for future education

We would like to think that our views are not just our own fantasies, but that they find some common ground with others. Likewise, we think that schools should fit with the society they serve and so, designing schools for the future should be done with the expected developments of society in mind. The problem is, although some may claim to have, none of us can prove in advance to possess, precognition. A well known method of a more reasoned nature in dealing with future uncertainty is the development of scenarios: likely possible future developments drawn from current trends and our expectations. We tend to put more trust in scenarios if they are backed by acknowledged experts (as it is with a lot of information).

For your consideration, we wish to present two sets of scenarios, developed by others, independently. Scenarios are designed around axes indicating the two extreme outcomes of a trend or development. When two or more axes are combined this results in scenario spaces where for each trend or axis, a choice has been made regarding its direction leading to the respective scenario.

Figure 6.1 shows a well known quadrant of scenarios, often described as the 'Edinburgh scenarios' presented by the Scottish Enterprise. These scenarios were developed in the

Figure 6.1 The Edinburgh scenarios

months leading up to the eLearn International 2004 summit, held in Edinburgh. The two trends chosen (Figure 6.2) to form the Edinburgh scenarios are, on the one hand, the role of technology in society and, consequently, the speed of adoption of new technology and, on the other hand, the balance of power in society, driving stability and change. The scenarios try to paint a picture of what society would be like if the changes of today would continue their trend and we were to consider two variables, the two axes. At the extremes of both axes we would find four scenarios, which we will briefly discuss.

On the lower left of Figure 6.1 is what was called 'Back to the future'. Imagine if the role of technology in society would remain a source of frustration for most. People would not want technology because it would require that they learn how to use it, but also, quite too often, how to resolve its problems. Unreliable technology is useless, so only proven and long tested technology would find a way into our daily lives. With society clinging to certainty in times of change, the traditional powers would retain their influence and suppress the emergence of new initiatives. The consequence – learning would be much like it is today; learning experiences would be predictable, managed and standard.

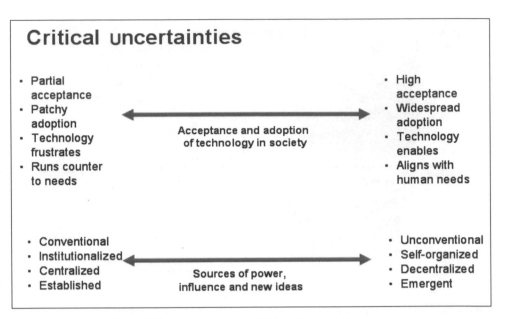

Figure 6.2 The axes for the Edinburgh scenarios

In contrast, if we were to accept technological uncertainty and start experimenting and using a lot of the new inventions early in their development, we could see rapid technological progress. With established institutions and corporations still maintaining momentum, we would see technology mainly being used for efficiency gains, with a few major players dominating the market and setting standards. They labelled this scenario, 'Virtually vanilla'. This scenario would see learners reaping the benefits of technology in their learning because more efficient learning would embrace the principles of 'any time, any place'.

Diagonally across, when fear of technology persists but individual opportunities leave room for change, a scenario of 'You choose' is envisioned. Technology would be feared and not widely used. Established powers would be mistrusted and people would retreat into comfortable local communities for their trusted environment. Because of differences in needs, beliefs and experiences, there would be a wide variety of uses of technology in education by different cultures and communities. People would be looking for new educational models and formats, being unsatisfied with established practices.

Now, if we were to embrace technological and societal change and immerse ourselves completely in the opportunities surrounding us, we might see society moving towards a 'web of confidence'. Society would slowly transform under the growing influence of technology as it has been doing for some time. The importance of internet communities for people's everyday lives would increase, allowing people to break with old constructs. Global communication would increasingly erase geographical barriers and as information can be supplied and accessed by anyone, each individual would need to develop the skills to discern the value of information. What is important, valuable and true would become a matter of negotiation and so it can be said that knowledge, as the product of valuation of information, resides in networks of communication between individuals. The globe would increasingly be interconnected and your network would consist of whom you trust and confide in. Education would see the benefits of changing technology and emerging initiatives to create diversity and choice, making learning a sought after, fun and individual experience.

From the above four scenarios, it may already be clear that none will come to pass completely and we can see small measures of each scenario already taking effect in today's world. Indeed, this is the strength of scenario development: it allows you a framework to choose which changes you think are most important and to follow them through in a 'what if' supposition to discover their possible implications. Choosing which direction you think change is most likely to take us, you will at least have a marker to start shaping your decisions.

Before we comment on the scenarios of others and explain our choices, consider the following different set of scenarios. These scenarios were developed for the E-merge consortium. E-merge is a consortium of a number of institutions in higher education in the Netherlands, including Delft University of Technology. E-merge aims to further co-operation in the field of technological facilitation of education (ICT in education). A few years ago, the constituting partners commissioned a scenario study as a basis for further policy and research (van Staalduinen, 2004). As with the Edinburgh scenarios, the study included a review of trends and most likely options by experts; this eventually led to the scenarios shown in Figure 6.3.

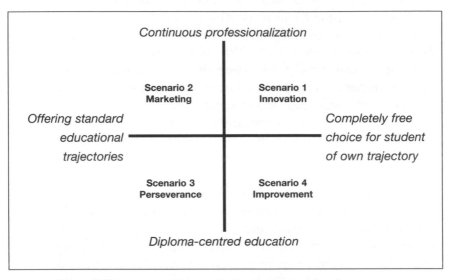

Figure 6.3 E-merge scenarios for the future of education

The first significant trend that was discerned in this research is whether education will relinquish control of learning trajectories to the individual learners or retain control of curricula on an institutional level. The second trend is the continuity of learning taking place in an individual's lifetime: we could see lifelong learning or diploma-centred educational packages as two extremes of this axis. In contrast to the Edinburgh scenarios, you may notice how this research takes technological progress and adoption for granted. Designing four scenarios around choice of educational trajectories and the needs in society with respect to learning, we arrive at the following four options.

Again, in the lower left corner of Figure 6.3 we see scenario 3 labelled 'Perseverance'. Through the progress of technology, the E-merge consortium would maintain an offering of standard educational trajectories in fixed packages, much like most of education today. The influence of technology would be limited to increasing the efficiency of education, with electronic environments easing the administration and distribution of traditional education. You might easily see the resemblance between this scenario and the scenario of 'Virtually vanilla'.

To the right of this we see scenario 4, that of 'Improvement'. Accepting a large degree of freedom for students to make their own career choices, it would be logical to allow them the same degree of freedom in choosing their curricula. To enable a diversified offering of education, technology would be used to develop new formats of education and make existing offerings more effective. Students would still receive some form of certification, and after completing their own chosen path of education, they would enter working life with a specialized set of personal skills.

Following trends in the opposite direction brings scenario 2, that of 'Marketing'. Realizing that learning does not stop after the age of 25 (30 at most), higher education would drop the certification of fixed trajectories and start co-operating with corporations to offer networks of learning and, for instance, training events for corporate employees. The content of courses would continuously be kept current by educational institutions and companies would receive the best up-to-date training for their employees. Technology could serve to facilitate this exchange so that employees no longer need to take a week off to attend classes. Individual learners would have to select one of the many pre-chosen paths for developing themselves.

The last scenario in this set is labelled 'Innovation'. Not only will institutions accept the necessity of lifelong learning, but also pedagogy will have realized the need for demand driven, individual and diverse trajectories. Technology is used to enable both new formats and new networks of distribution as a fusion of the corporate and academic world leads to the creation of 'corporate-educational lifelong learning tracks'. Learning becomes state-of-the-art and personalized.

Other interesting sets of scenarios for the future of education include the OECD scenarios (2004), which can be found in the report, *Schooling for Tomorrow* and another set of scenarios developed by the National Education Association in the United States. A link for both is provided on our website (www.homozappiens.nl), where you're also welcome to add your own set of scenarios if you would like. The OECD report touches upon such aspects as 'extended adolescence' and the seemingly diminishing role for upfront education in society, the increased need to pay attention to knowing 'why, how and who', in addition to knowing 'what', and the role of schools in supporting community life and values. It identifies an axis of de-schooling, re-schooling or maintaining the status quo and establishes two scenarios for each. When maintaining the status quo, without problems worth mentioning, they predict an increase of ICT within existing structures to increase efficiency. A negative exponent of this scenario might be a shortage in teaching personnel, which would create a drain on funds and thus infrastructure and ICT innovation. Because of pressures on the system it may either break down or show some highly innovative responses.

Re-schooling is a trend where a new position for schools is created within society. This could focus on one of two things. Either schools are seen as a vital element in the social network and will develop to include more non-cognitive goals in their curricula, or schools will maintain a strong focus on knowledge and specialize as learning, researching organizations. Both scenarios would agree there is need for change in the current approach, but maintain that schools as institutions serve a purpose. Lastly, the report identifies two scenarios that recognize that the need for schooling institutions is declining. In a fifth scenario, learning networks would emerge in a network society, where authority and responsibility for schooling are shared among a community network. Obviously ICT would see extensive application to enable individualized learning arrangements and home schooling. A final scenario is identified where a de-schooling trend is driven by increased market influence. More suppliers of schooling enter a deregulated market and, as a result, the size of arrangements available will decrease to allow more diversity in learning routes. Corporate supply and demand may come to dominate the content of learning trajectories and the nature of assessment.

In the NEA scenarios (2006), this same axis of quality versus market is drawn. On the market driven side, educational systems may develop aspects such as an educational debit card (a card giving free access to a certain amount of learning), professionally trained presenters as lecturers, and dedicated researchers providing knowledge and outsourced teaching. They may also develop as a pyramid structured warehouse as increased scale for efficiency and a shortage in teaching personnel lead them to develop computer courses for the basic level of knowledge, with higher level students teaching lower level students until ultimately only the highest level students would be taught by faculty staff. In all aspects of education, teaching, content, administration and infrastructure, efficiency and outsourcing would be the norm, not the exception.

Quality driven scenarios centre around the belief that government should provide access to higher education for all (through loans). In these scenarios, we see a large amount of co-operation rising between institutes of higher education as together they try to handle the increase in student numbers. Students can earn extra years in education by performing community service. As a result of co-operation and efficiency, the highest level educational institutions will operate on a global scale and local infrastructure will serve only to facilitate lab work and a social environment; students would not need to travel to obtain a course from an overseas source. Workers, wanting to update their skills, will have access to a large repository of online material and consequently courses with widespread applicability will cost little to acquire, where more specialized knowledge has fewer buyers and a heftier price tag. Teacher shortages may be overcome by hiring retired professionals.

As a reflection on the above mentioned scenarios, we would like to offer you our view on and our choice of scenarios. Only the Edinburgh scenarios consider the possibility of a reluctant acceptance of ICT in society, where all the others consider technological progress a given, though its use may vary. As we already see *Homo zappiens* making their entrance in society and know this generation has absolutely no fear of technology, we suspect that it's rather likely that increased global co-operation and online networking will continue. We personally think that society will keep the role of seeing young members educated, although this need not necessarily be through institutions or government. Mostly though, what we as a society deem important will usually become (or remain) the responsibility of the government to enable and facilitate.

With the increased importance of learning in our economies, it is only natural that commercial organizations will increase their market share of instructional offerings. While (public) education may start looking for more diverse paths of instruction, each separate standard path may be offered more cheaply and more efficiently through training companies. In higher education, universities and the corporate world may well converge into one privately funded model of an educational institute as a social hub of researchers and experts. Primary, secondary and tertiary education will continue to mainly focus on developing a child's sense of self and surroundings. In early phases of development it's important that each person learns to recognize their own strengths and weaknesses, preferences and motivation. It's in this phase that (role-) play could become an excellent addition to knowledge instruction. From the age of 3–4 to age 18–21, education will slowly but gradually be supporting the individual with experiences in knowledge, skills and values to take charge of his or her direction in learning. We will continue to discuss the required elements for such education further on in this chapter.

The described scenarios all aim to predict the period from 2011–2020. They also share the fact that they're at the extremes of their contributing trends and will most likely not be realized in full. We think, for instance, in the case of the Edinburgh and E-merge scenarios, that society will move towards the upper right of the diagram, with educational systems resembling more a networked, diverse and innovative blend of academic and corporate settings. We think it's most likely, or at least preferred, that society develops a mix of schools and home-school initiatives, as some children will require discipline and others may simply need sufficient resources and little stimulation. Instead of certification, one might think of a personal career coach assessing children's choices and setting tasks in development.

Pedagogical design of future learning

Education has always been about preparing individuals for their role in society. Over the past decade, the primacy of formal education has fallen because we now see the emergence of lifelong learning and informal education, as new areas for learning take an ever larger part in individuals' lives. Forms of on the job training, personal development plans and competency courses for new managers have become commonplace in corporate environments. Gone are the times when graduating with a certain degree or diploma qualified you for certain jobs, but to say that education is necessarily doomed is an exaggeration. What has happened, in effect, is that society is now changing so fast with so much room for innovation and individual contributions that our old system of standards no longer suffices. As a result, many people with standard qualifications continue their specialization, developing their talents and skills while working.

In order for education to be able to deliver on the demands of tomorrow, teachers will have to take a fresh look at their jobs in leading our youth to become a knowledgeable and valuable contribution to society. Instead of shielding children from the big bad world, children should be encouraged to explore this world with a lifeline, only to flee back to safety when needed. Most children will prove far more inquisitive and exploring than their parents would feel at ease with, but this is the phase in their life when they learn the most. Why would we restrain them? If the answer to this question is negative, what would be the major principles on which our future education should focus? What general design principles should underpin our education system? Below, we present seven design principles for future education (Veen & Jacobs, 2005). They do not specifically refer to the uses of technology in education. However, they are generic principles that are far better to achieve when using technology.

The first major principle in designing future education is **trust**. Not just the trust a student needs to experiment safely or the trust one needs to accept information as accurate, but most importantly the trust a teacher needs to have that his student will learn. Traditional education has been a system of mistrust, taking for granted that children should be controlled, and assessed on their shortcomings rather than on their achievements. Hardly surprising then that when classes come to an end, students rush out of the classroom and leave school as soon as possible. To the contrary, I recently came across a Dutch school where students protested against the school closing for holidays! That was quite an experience; students willing to come to school to meet each other and learn. I must say this school is an innovative school where intrinsic motivation is the driving force for learning. But consider another lack of trust when children who were labelled ignorant, even stupid, before society understood dyslexia; or children even now, who suffer from ADD (attention deficit disorder), who may very well be labelled lazy or a nuisance and required to attend special schooling because they're unmanageable in most classes. *Homo zappiens* are also mistrusted as many teachers still think they are copying information from the net and learning superficially. Lack of trust between teachers and students inhibits motivation and makes learning more difficult.

Suppose you let a class of young children decide how and when they finish their assignments, with you simply present to assist them should they ask for help. After a few days you may see that a few need a little extra guidance still, but how many will surprise you by completing their tasks sooner than expected and having time free for them to explore in new ways? Trust your children or students not to be stupid, even intelligent and they might just surprise you. Trust that your children are learning when they play or communicate, even if it may not be apparent to you, and ask them to explain what they've learned.

A second principle for future education is **relevance**. To understand this consider your own youth: when did you really start to appreciate history or geography or maths? –

when you understood its relevance and recognized its use in your daily life! Perhaps when you suddenly understood your grandfather's mood when he talked about the war, or when you were able to predict how long a car journey to visit your uncle would take. Is it not amazing that children who do poorly in maths at school have no trouble at all playing a simulation game, such as Roller Coaster Tycoon, which is basically nothing more than a spreadsheet full of formulas and numbers. Would they be better in the game if they knew maths? Maybe; would they do better in maths if someone told them they are already doing the same thing in a computer game? Most likely! The principle of relevance goes beyond offering the appropriate content to connect with students' experience; it's about offering relevance in the methods of instruction and assessment as well.

Let us use the example of two children to demonstrate the third important element. One child is an intellectual, who loves to solve puzzles and mathematical problems. The other loves to work with his hands. They both attended the same primary school where teachers already noticed this difference. Yet, both arrive at the same high school and end up taking the same classes in the first year because the government has decided so. Would it be such a big surprise to tell you that the first child does very well in theoretical and abstract courses and is mostly in his element, while the other is seriously demotivated by school except for the one technical hands on course taught? What education has done for decades is finding someone's weaknesses and patching them. Sure enough, someone who excels in maths may have had some freedom to finish all materials sooner, but education focused on their weakness in grammar. We wanted so much that 'no one was to be left behind' that we neglected to recognize that there may be different paths to a productive future.

The third element of future education is, in short, **talent**. If you discover someone's talents and focus on developing them, instead of trying to patch all the 'gaps', you will have far greater success in your teaching, since talents are those aspects in a human being where he or she may outperform the average. Usually the individual knows this on some subconscious level and is therefore also better motivated.

If you ask young *Homo zappiens* why they play computer games for hours on end, you would expect to hear the answer, fun. When we did ask them, they actually said, **challenge**. They play because the game challenges them! They can focus and concentrate on one thing because it challenges them. All the while we may have been wondering why the same *Homo zappiens* are so distracted in class or in college seats during lectures. Students at Delft University of Technology recently said about lectures that only 10 per cent of most lectures is important information and that they've usually already forgotten half of what was said by the time they leave the room (Veen & Vrakking, 2006)! Compare this to children in school who start talking to their classmates during lessons, stare out of the window or take their books and prepare for their next class. All because what is being said is not interesting enough or, in other words, the information density of the medium is too low. What education should do is offer truly complex problems for each individual. In line with the other principles, these must tap into their talents, resemble the real world around them and should leave room for each child to fail and seek help. Challenge your children and students!

The next two pedagogical design principles may follow logically from the previous four. If you want children to be challenged, to give them room to fail, to trust them and to provide them with relevance and focus according to their talents, all you really need to do is immerse them and follow their passion. **Immersion** is what they experience in computer games. They enter virtual worlds and become part of them. *Immersion* is very important for students and not really that hard to do. Instead of feeding your students with step-by-step lessons in a foreign language let them immerse themselves in a learning environment, such as multimedia resources, and let them work for hours and days. Language teachers have assured me that learning a foreign language can be easily done without any grammar during the first two years of study. A limited number of schools have adopted this immersion approach for modern language teaching, and meanwhile most of the Dutch students have learned English this way by playing computer games and watching television. They are experienced in English far more than we were when we were at school. Their immersion consisted of starting playing games, having to read texts while listening to the sound track. No easy stepping stone approaches, just immersion.

Passion is something they will have to bring. If someone is not passionate about something, they usually haven't had a trigger experience to recognize what they feel strongly about. Children who have no passion deserve most of your attention, to help them to bring it out. This is also where discovering their talents is involved. Someone will usually feel passionate about something they do particularly well and they will develop something particularly well if they feel passionate about it. For those students who already have a passion, all we need to do is tap into it. For example, if we want a fashion conscious girl to learn about maths, about Fibonacci numbers, why should we not ask her to design a piece of clothing or even a collection of clothing in which she demonstrates this knowledge and throw in a mandatory style for challenge, say, the late eighteenth century French haute couture. Let us make her use design software and ask her to show us ten examples of similarly designed clothing before she begins. She will be combining maths, French, computer sciences and art history and all the while doing something she is passionate about. She will be exploring these fields of knowledge and, along the way, may find that there is much more for her to learn. Of all design principles, passion may be the key to motivation and motivation, as we should all know, is the key to learning.

Now, all of the above may seem difficult to bring about. How should you provide a class of 30 with assignments and learning tailored to their talents and passion, make it relevant, challenging and immersive enough to capture their attention and motivation; how can you possibly trust all of them to learn, to come to you for guidance? How can you manage 30 different individual leads? The answer is *self-direction*, the seventh principle. But in order to give control to students, teachers cannot continue to take sole responsibility for what happens in the classroom. Students also need to take responsibility as they take control of their own learning trajectories. Teachers can coach them, offer them experience and knowledge if they decide to come and get it, and monitor their progress, but if they fail or decide that the road they have taken is not the right one, this is their responsibility. They will not fail in life because of it; instead they may need to take some extra time to develop a missing competence before embarking upon the right road for them.

Many adults may encounter exactly the same problem, but when they do there is usually no educational system to guide them and they must solve their problems on their own or seek help. These children would be fortunate that they have a parent or a teacher to watch out for them, but all the while they should be learning to deal with problems as will be expected from them as adults. *Homo zappiens* want to take control of their learning process; this is what they do all day when classes have come to an end. It would not be strange to them if schools would organize self-direction in a way that students can learn at the pace they want, in the place they want and with whom they want.

Changes in schools

What of standards, requirements, curricula, qualifications, you may say? What of traditional schools, with classes and courses and dedicated teachers? What of universities with lecturers, bachelors, masters and scientific responsibilities? We said it before and we'll say it again: if you do not believe change is the way to go, if you think what we have now is what we will ever need, do not look any further. Yet somehow, we do not believe you would be reading this chapter, nor this book, if you didn't think the future might have something better to offer us. To those looking for solutions, for change, we must disappoint you: we do not have one clear-cut solution; you will have to find what fits you best. What we can offer is five elements of current 'traditional' schooling that may be obsolete; five major fundamental choices to be made when designing your school's approach to the future. These fundamental choices all relate to flexibility. Flexibility of learning activities, of content, of grouping and of pacing. Information technology enables schools to make these choices and redesign their organization. The choices are: (a) year programmes, (b) exams, (c) curricula, (d) time slots and (e) separated subjects.

Schools have set standards, thresholds if you wish, which children must pass to advance to the next level or year. This is very easy if you wish to keep a uniform group of comparable knowledge, for instance, to teach them a next level of standard maths. At some point in time, we thought it would be necessary for children to first know the alphabet before they learned how to read. However, consider what a dyslexic child will have to suffer if it fails to learn the alphabet along with its classmates? It will have to remain in Year 1 while all its buddies advance, yet it was the best pupil in maths and by far the best artist in the classroom. Now 80 per cent of what it will be taught is already known; maybe in a good school they will allow this child to take extra time to study letters, but this could most certainly have been done just as well without breaking up a social group and blocking progress in maths or art.

Consider how some children may be far ahead of others in reading, writing or maths, but lack the sensory motor skills for creative activities. Others may have a natural ability in dance, theatre, music, fashion or humour and social skills. Why should one child be fit for more advanced tuition and why do we not recognize the others' special talents? Why as a society do we demand that every one of them is capable in every subject, instead of stimulating them to excel in a few and allowing them to leave other skills for later development as he or she needs them?

One of the first choices we propose that education makes is to drop the **programming of years**. If we demand that every child develop a certain level of, for example, maths, writing, reading and art at a certain age, we do not leave room for some abilities to develop faster than others. As a consequence, we're not adhering to the design principles for future education that prescribe self-direction, passion and talent. The consequences of dropping the programming of years could be that children aged ten and six acquire the same level of proficiency in maths, with the six year old teaching the ten year old. The other way around, the ten year old may be teaching the six year old about language or other experiences which naturally come with age. We should gradually come to realize that older does not always imply senior in every way. Teachers and students sometimes switch places, for instance, when it comes to computers nowadays, and maybe it's time that we allow for this mutually beneficial contact.

A second choice, which is closely related to the programming of years, is the **standard exams**. Because, as a society, we still demand diplomas and exams, educational institutions have to implement some build-up towards these final certifications. What we want in society is some way to compare people with each other, but what we have now is a system to compare everyone with an ideal standard. This standard can only function if there is an average and that implies that at least *half* of those measured perform below average. No room for different, diverse or better suited in other areas; we have people perform below average! And how do we go about solving this problem? We lower and change our standards so that the mandatory threshold is sufficiently below average so that almost everyone can leave secondary school with at least some exams. Then we say that, as a society, we have done our educational task and it's now up to the individual, when in fact we have done little but test if someone is able in a limited number of expertises.

If we, as a society, continue demanding that children learn to discover and develop their talents and their potential from an early age; if we want people to specialize in what they truly feel passionate about and where they excel, then we should provide the room to choose and diverge. We should drop our standard certification and allow for other forms of measuring quality. A few examples of alternatives might be a job test, a portfolio or entry exam. All of these alternatives place choice and responsibility with the learner, the applicant. If you think you've finished your education with sufficient result, you can apply for an entry qualification to a university or apply for a job and have the company determine your aptitude, either through your portfolio or an in-house assessment. Many of these tests are already in place; many companies and universities already have entry qualification tests to deal with the diversity in national or university curricula. Yet somehow, we have taken it upon ourselves to relieve the majority of companies and universities from these assessments by taking them into the public domain and labelling them 'exams'. While noble the cause may be we also eliminated the room for divergence. As a result, someone who has problems and drops out of school has little chance of reaching his fullest potential even if he may want to. How much would society be wasting?

On to a third principle: one size fits all **curricula**. If (final) exams are a measure of assessment in society, then curricula are the specification of the standard. Now, there is in itself nothing wrong with specifying a standard. It's even beneficial for most purposes. So then, the part we must be objecting against is the 'one size fits all' notion and indeed, reader, you are right! Call us preachers of new education or just ordinary human beings with an image of a better future, but diversity is part of our message. If we want to allow trust, relevance, talent, challenge, immersion, passion and self-direction in education, we cannot do so without diversity. One standard curriculum simply will no longer do. This is not to say that there are not already many alternatives. Look at colleges and universities; look at corporate training academies or professional training consultants. There is a great variety in courses offered. Yet we have not brought this level down to the individual because this makes administration a little bit more difficult.

If we stopped considering this barrier from a focal point of control and started looking at it from a point of facilitation, we might allow ourselves to see the possible solutions already available to us. Students could, for instance, become the record keepers of their own achievements and this is the only really different solution. Any system which looks at it from a control perspective, where teachers dole out credits for courses taken, will inevitably pull towards an economy of scale, where the registration process is centralized and thus either incredibly labour intensive or bound to standards.

Fourth in our series of educational choices for innovation is the **time slot**, usually of 45 or 50 minutes. We just need to look at our own adult lives to understand how utterly silly this is. When you learn a language, do you measure progress in intervals of 45 minutes? When you write a report, do you measure deadlines in multiples of 45 minutes? If you want to make a painting, do you call it done after 50 minutes? No, you don't. Indeed, this is also the case in schools. Most assignments are not finished within 45–50 minutes. That is why we know the concept of homework.

Now consider yourself having a day off. You sit at breakfast, sipping your coffee, reading the newspaper and musing over what to do with your day. Do you all of a sudden get up, go to the garage to get your bike and go training? Do you time your training to be exactly one and a half hours so you can be on time to start painting? Do you cut off your telephone conversation at noon because you have to pick up your online Spanish course? Most importantly, if you did, would it make you feel satisfied and fulfilled or rushed and incomplete?

Mostly, we set between three and seven goals for ourselves in a day and we take our best estimate of the time required to assess whether this is reasonable. We then plan and measure progress by results. Why should we teach our children differently? Would they not also see this discrepancy? If we split the day into blocks of 45 minutes to give them small breaks, why do we have them rush to their next class? Why not let them decide for themselves if they need those breaks and whether they want to change activities with each time slot.

Learning is a process that takes time; sometimes it takes more time for one individual to learn something. Completing assignments in one's own time is not a problem, but why should we not consider all the time spent in school as 'one's own time'. If we must divide time into blocks, the only logical split is the lunch break. There is no logical reason why children should suddenly do something very different from the morning activity after lunch. So, concerning time slots, maybe we should consider abandoning them altogether or we could make a more logical or rhythmic planning over the year.

Having considered year programmes, standard exams, curricula and time slots, there is one more choice, we think, that has a great impact on how education will be received. This fifth choice to be made by current education is whether or not to drop the **separated subjects**. Why teach biology, chemistry, physics and maths as separate subjects when, in real life, these fields are combined in disciplines of purpose, for instance, nanotechnology or biomechanical engineering. Why teach art and history separate from languages or maths? Why have both economics, and management and organization? If this is just our current way of making theory more manageable, more approachable for students, then surely there must be alternatives.

As scientists specialize, their field of expertise narrows and so it makes sense to have them teach only their limited bit of expertise. At the same time, this would mean that we have literally hundreds of thousands of small subjects to teach. Looking at secondary schools today, it's often the fact that the same teachers who teach biology or physics also teach chemistry. So it would make perfect sense to combine the topics too, would it not? There is another reason for dropping strict barriers between courses in favour of more logical ones and this is the practical implementation of projects in education: it's far easier to hand out relevant, immersive, tailored assignments to students that challenge them to demonstrate the similarities and applicability of each for a certain topic. Almost no project in the real world is merely concerned with one scientific discipline. As for language, it's much easier to learn when practised, for instance, while working on a project about foreign culture and history.

Above is what we consider to be the building blocks for new education and new schools. It can be difficult to imagine all of the above suddenly changing, especially when entire organizations and numerous teaching personnel have been accustomed to a system of control for so long. Unless we start building schools from the ground up, with people who are willing to fit into a new organization, we will have a slow road of change ahead of us. As long as we keep in mind why we are pushing for these changes and what it is we want to achieve, we can think of ways to gradually alter our organizations and build new networks of students and teachers, mentors and pupils. A network of learning that does not distinguish between age or degree, but rather considers every individual on his or her merits, skills and competences.

Examples of current best practices

Educational institutions that have embraced even one of these constructs can be called innovative, because they all tie together. If you really want to implement one of the seven described principles or fully support one of the five organizational choices, you will, sooner or later, be confronted with restrictions on the others. So, ultimately, when you set in motion the wheels of progress, you will continuously face the choice 'stop or go further'. Let us proceed by showing you some examples of these principles already happening right now, drawing on an interesting article by Martine Zuidweg (translated by Raymond Gijsen) published in October 2002, about an experimental school then just started: Slash21. It's a good illustration of the problems and choices facing secondary education in the Netherlands then, but we think it's of equal relevance to many schools, in the Netherlands and abroad, today.

Innovative learning in secondary education

At /21 (Slash21) in Lichtenvoorde (a small Dutch town between Arnhem and the German border), most teaching materials are provided by computer. No homework, no books. Pupils compose their own study plan. Three months focusing on one foreign language, then three months learning another one. Tutors assist and motivate. Is /21 the school of the future?

At /21, children don't buy books. There are no classrooms and none of the traditional fields to study. And neither are school days split up into the traditional 50 minute lessons. "The school of the future," a regional newspaper headlined when the plans for /21 were first announced.

Doreen Wieggers (aged 12) is a pupil at /21. She says students at the nearby Marianum College are green with envy, and particularly her brother, who is a pupil in fourth grade at Marianum College. "When my parents send him upstairs to go and do his homework, he gives me this really foul look." But there's also envy over the large number of computers at /21. This school has six computers for every ten pupils. The school started two weeks ago [mid-September 2002]. But Doreen still has the feeling that she hasn't properly started school yet. Her friend, who's studying at Marianum College, went to pick up her books on her first day of the new term – and was ready for lessons. "We were not," Doreen says. "We first had to find out what exactly we were supposed to be doing."

Tutors instead of teachers

The school curriculum at /21 is not only decided by teachers. The students also have to take responsibility for their own education. At /21, you don't see children behind neat rows of desks, all facing the standard blackboard at the front of the classroom. There are no bags full of books on the floor either. Each grade has a large room with a number of islands – desks with computers arranged in circles – where groups of children work on specific assignments. Each month, all students compose their own study plans. In these plans, they specify what they will be doing next month on a particular theme or the foreign language they're studying. In these study plans, children also specify what hasn't worked well for them in the previous month and how they intend to tackle the problem. For each child, the school has an electronic progress overview ("portfolio"), in which the children themselves record what they are working on. Parents with a connection to the internet can consult their own child's portfolio.

Slash21 is an initiative launched by the Carmel College Foundation, a regional school board responsible for 21 secondary level schools. The school has been set up in association with "KPC Group", an educational consultancy company. Carmel and KPC wanted to bring about a real change in Dutch secondary level education. Many parents also clearly felt things had to change: /21 immediately received 190 applications. "It's remarkable that so many people would opt for the uncertainty of a new school in a region which isn't exactly known as progressive," says the school's director, Henk van Dieten. Van Dieten was an educational adviser to the Carmel College Foundation and helped develop the educational concept for the new school.

At /21, teachers are called tutors. And for a reason, because teachers at /21 don't teach, but instead assist, stimulate and observe. Each incoming year is assigned a team of tutors and educational assistants that will remain with that group of pupils as it moves from first through third grade. Hence, each child has the same mentors for three years running. The tutors really had to get used to working in teams, Van Dieten says. "Teachers are used to working individually. Here they work in groups of ten, assisting groups of 50 pupils. That's really a major change."

Working in teams of tutors and assistants has the advantage that the staff can correct each other, says educational assistant Mark Lankveld. "Sometimes, we find ourselves pointing out really simple things to one another – for example, telling a colleague to look in different directions while explaining something, to make sure everyone in the class can hear what he says." Another advantage of working in teams is that no time is lost when one of the assistants falls ill. Parents don't have to be afraid that, in the event of a member of the staff suddenly being absent, their children will get an hour off and go wandering about in the school's neighbourhood or are sent home early. All pupils remain in the school grounds from 9:30am to 3:30pm. /21 has an intensive foreign language education programme.[1] For 12 weeks running, pupils will spend four morning or afternoon sessions on one specific foreign language. Native speakers

---

[1] In Dutch schools, the foreign language curriculum typically comprises English, French and German.

are in attendance. After three months, the children will switch to another foreign language, again concentrating on it for three months running. Dutch is not taught at the school, at least not as a separate subject.

Ivar Gierveld, until recently a teacher of Dutch at the (nearby) Marianum College, has no issue with that at all. "Of course at the end of their school period, they will have to be able to analyse and summarize texts – but you don't need separate Dutch lessons to develop those skills. It's something children can also acquire when working on a specific theme – gradually."

Themes instead of subjects

At /21, pupils work in groups on themes, such as "power" or "energy". By studying themes, they have to draw on knowledge from various fields. Physics, mathematics, chemistry and biology are not taught as separate subjects, but rather as elements of more comprehensive, overarching concepts. In order to explain a specific topic, teachers will of course resort to handbooks every now and then, but most educational material is made available electronically. Being dependent on technology has had the drawback of making the school more vulnerable, as Van Dieten has found out. During the first couple of weeks, systems broke down repeatedly.

The main disadvantage of an electronic teaching environment, however, is the lack of content, particularly on overarching themes comprising different subjects. "It's the typical 'chicken or the egg problem'," says Van Dieten. The major publishers of education material don't produce what we need because there's no market for it. The market, in turn, is reluctant to adopt this kind of teaching method because there's not enough content on offer." KPC Group is now finalizing a programme that aligns closely with one of the main principles of the school: empowering pupils to influence their own learning processes.

An electronic learning environment is expensive. The Carmel College Foundation and KPC Group are investing several million euros in developing /21. Part of the money is provided by the Dutch Ministry of Education's "Curriculum Development Foundation" and various businesses sponsoring the initiative.[2] "At the moment, we have higher costs than schools on average, but this will change. We expect that, a few years from now, our cost level will be in line with that of other schools," says Van Dieten.

Is /21 indeed the school of the future? Only time will tell. Many elements of the new model will gradually unfold in practice, after a couple of months working with it Van Dieten says, "We're launching a completely new company, as it were. We have lots of little flaws, but we will iron them out." One of the tutors at the school, Kees Heemskerk, agrees. Until recently, he taught at another school in the region. "At /21, the future is far from clear," he says. It's all so very new and totally different from anything he had grown accustomed to. However, the very fact that /21 does things differently is also what makes the school attractive. Heemskerk thinks it's high time that the first three years of the six year secondary level education system should change. "Most pupils are bored to death at school. Their main focus of attention is the next break between lessons. That really says it all, doesn't it?"

Thinking in pictures

ICT is very well suited for explaining phenomena, says the man responsible for the concept behind /21, the educationalist Harry Gankema of KPC Group. "I can tell you exactly what high and low tides are, but when the (educational) television programme shows an animation of high and low tides, the information will stick much better. That's because people think in images rather than rules or laws. Schools traditionally communicate in language, but people think in pictures."[3]

Gankema feels the traditional education system is dominated far too much by language. "Teachers tend to use language to describe phenomena, such as high and low tide. At /21, we would try to explain visually what they are,

[2] Financial and content sponsors are listed on the school's website, http://www.slash21.nl. Once on the home page, scroll down to the heading 'Samenwerking bedrijfsleven' on the right-hand side of the page, and click on 'Meer informatie'. If you require more information, please send an email to hdieten@marianum.nl.

because that way, children will understand it much better. Small wonder. If you're at the IKEA (assemble-it-yourself) furniture store, and they hand you a box with no more than the manual for putting together the contents of the box, you would have a hard time understanding what exactly the box entails. Add a picture of the final assembled product and things immediately get a whole lot easier."

Tapping a variety of sources is a good thing in knowledge transfer anyway, Gankema feels. At traditional schools, teachers and school books tend to be the only sources of information. Pupils are fed information as and when the teacher is ready to do so, or when the school book says it's time for another dose. Whether or not pupils are ready for it is not taken into consideration. "Most children make a leap in their development during their holidays. That's when they clearly learn new things, and without teachers," Gankema says. He expects pupils to learn much more if they are allowed to manage their own learning process.

In that respect, the educational system at /21 somewhat resembles the Montessori approach to teaching, while working in groups of pupils is reminiscent of the 'Jenaplan' approach.[4] Gankema: "I've taken the bits and pieces from the various trends in education psychology that are relevant for schools today, based on an analysis of the elements that, in practice, seem to be working well."

Effective learning also means that children grasp how different phenomena are related. Standard education, split up in separate subjects, doesn't do that. Gankema adds, "If we provide knowledge in separate bits and pieces, children often don't see that different phenomena are connected." Hence, /21 doesn't teach subject fields but instead focuses the curriculum on core terms or themes. "Take a theme, such as energy, for example," says Gankema. "If you want to get

[3] The German Panzer ace, Heinz Guderian, understood this some 60 years ago (and others in various professional fields before and after him, too, presumably) – according to some websites on Guderian, he threw out the bulky operating manuals for his Panzer crews and replaced them with manuals that looked more like comic books. Some of the material apparently was of the X-rated type, presumably as a consequence of the 'audience analysis' that went into the development effort.

[4] Montessori – education method named after Italian Maria Montessori – in the Netherlands typically applied in (some) primary schools; Jenaplan – also an educational method used in some Dutch schools.

a grasp of a concept like that, you have to know about physics, mathematics, chemistry and biology. Looking at things this way means that knowledge isn't split up."[5]

Final thought

Now, we do not expect you to digest one article to prove our intended point of feasibility. Not even if we mention that several other schools, such as Impuls, De Nieuwste School, Vathorst College, School of the Future, IJburg College or Amadeus College have now also started to offer similar innovative education programmes for the first years of secondary education. Higher education is also considering major initiatives, such as the Massachusetts Institute of Technology that has implemented the Open Course Ware Initiative – a free online service where most of the reading materials and lecture notes of their courses (about 1,700) are available for anyone, anywhere. Not to mention the Open University UK and NL who have come out with similar systems, providing repositories and depositories for free educational content as of October 2006. Depositories will be open for users to upload content creating communities of learners contributing to the body of knowledge of specific fields of study.

Even if we note that it's interesting to see how multinational corporations break in their management trainees, how plumbers coach apprentices on the job and how hairstylists learn by doing, we will not expect you to take these examples at face value and implement them right away. We expect you to go out and look for the seven proposed design principles in the most effective courses you know. Look for traces of our five choices for education in society. See for yourself how immersive learning is taking place every day and come to realize that, indeed, less than half of what children learn is learned in school.

---

[5] This 'holistic' approach to education (themes instead of specialized subjects) appears in line with the (then novel) teaching methods introduced at Maastricht University in the Netherlands when it started some 25 years ago (with a Medical School).

If you take what we have written in this book as a first pointer, you will see many changes in the world around you, in your children, your pupils or students and you may come to see for yourself how to fit in the changes we propose. You may even come up with new approaches and aspects of teaching and learning which we have not touched upon in this book. If you do, share them with us and others, like you, looking for a way to meet change head-on.

www.homozappiens.nl

We have written this book to offer a different and positive view on the changes confronting society, to show you challenging pictures of the *Homo zappiens*, a generation that provides us with opportunities for innovative teaching. We have tried to inspire you as a professional to consider reshaping the future of learning, taking into account well established design principles and choices. Information and communication technologies will profoundly change the way we learn as will society as a whole as it develops towards a creative knowledge intensive economy. In this society knowledge will be distributed and discontinued in technical and human networks. For learners knowledge creation will be a matter of aggregation rather than memorization. This very fact of distribution and discontinuity of knowledge leads us to think that eduation systems will change and teachers will be challenged as individual professionals to contribute to the implementation of those changes.

Glossary

Adventure games
A limited form of RPG (role-playing game), where the player has to follow a puzzle or quest to completion.

Blog
Short for weblog. A format for online periodic publishing, much like an online form of a diary, with the person maintaining it responsible for publishing new articles, images or references to other information. It has the main advantage of offering others, who may read these articles, the option to comment on them, again, for all to see.

Chat (room)
Online meeting space, frequently requiring the use of special software called IRC (Internet Relay Chat). It's specifically designed as a real time forum so that any participant entering can immediately see what others are contributing.

Cheat site
A site that provides gamers with 'cheat codes' or cheating software for various computer games. Both can be used to alter aspects of the game. Sometimes the game designer has enabled certain cheat codes, which have to be earned or may be publicly disclosed. In other cases a piece of software may be written that taps into the game and alters its behaviour. 'Cheats' are generally used to advance to a spot

in the game by a different course than intended by the game designer. Common examples of cheat codes are codes to give unlimited health, unlimited ammo, all possible items, as well as more basic codes to eliminate just one opponent or open a door or level.

Compression algorithm

A compression algorithm is a method for selecting and removing unnecessary bits from an object to reduce the required space for storage. The algorithm should also provide a means for restoring the object to its usable state. Squeezing a plastic bag to remove the air is an example. In terms of computers consider compression of files. There exist many different compression algorithms all tailored to specific purposes. For instance, MP3 is a method for removing unused bits and inaudible frequencies from music streams to reduce the necessary storage space by as much as 900 per cent. RAR or ZIP are common methods for compressing any type of file, although they may not be as efficient as a specifically tailored algorithm.

Creative Commons

Creative Commons is an alternative to the 'all rights restricted' intellectual property rights. Authors can decide, for instance, to allow free use, copying, or modification as long as their copyright is mentioned. See http://creativecommons.org for more information.

CTRL-F   [Control and F key]

Denotes the keystrokes made on a computer keyboard that, in most cases, invoke a search action for the user to make the computer scan through lines of text, looking for the keywords. Similar examples include CTRL-C for copy and CTRL-V for paste, a combination frequently used when moving or duplicating data.

Discontinuous information

Refers to information coming in bits and pieces instead of a continuous stream. Often, pieces may be missing. Unlike storylines being told in books, films and theatre plays, the perceivers of discontinuous information will have to use one of their own frameworks or models for puzzling together the data to extract information. Almost everyone possesses the skill to process discontinuous information to some extent, with more need and skill arising when the amount and diversity of information increases.

e-Learning

This is used both as a term for electronically supported learning as well as various formats for delivering learning content. Because of a huge hype, frequently leading to expectations being too high, e-learning has also acquired some very negative connotations. As with any format or content delivery, the process surrounding e-learning is paramount to its success.

Forum

Online discussion board on the internet. A forum is a means for asynchronous communication, that is, people do not have to be online at the same time for the communication. A forum may be created to discuss any number of topics and can store all previous communications, neatly sorted into categories and 'threads' (chains of a starting remark and all ensuing comments). This makes forums the ideal tool with which to provide users with FAQ lists: frequently asked questions and their answers.

Game console

Describes a computer platform that was designed for the sole purpose of playing games. Often connected to a television set for viewing, popular examples include competing brands, such as, Nintendo Gamecube, Sony Playstation and Microsoft Xbox.

Homo zappiens

Name chosen by Wim Veen and Ben Vrakking for the generation of children, born after 1990, who have never known a world without the internet and technology. Seeing technology and the internet as a natural extension of their environment, they are not obsessed with mastering, fearing or controlling technology: they expect it to be available and make use of whatever works best. Growing up in times of change and information abundance, they have developed strategies for communication, co-operation and handling information, which may prove crucial for society in decades to come. Since they are used to collaboration, exploration and experimentation, traditional schooling seems to be an exceptionally poor fit for their needs; *Homo zappiens* have been known to consider school 'outside the real world'.

Hyperlink

A hyperlink is a reference. It can take the form of an underlined word in a piece of text or an image that you can click on with your mouse. Hyperlinks can refer to another part of the same text or resource or can point you to different resources. Hyperlinks are the threads that tie millions of separate resources together on the internet.

iPod

Brand name for one of the most popular digital portable media playback devices on the market today. Sold by Apple Computer, Inc., it's mainly used for playing MP3s. Other emerging uses include the playback of video files and podcasting, the distribution of multimedia content to other iPod users.

LimeWire (*see* P2P)

MMO(RP)G – (Massively Multiplayer Online (Role-Playing) Game)

An online gaming environment in which many players assume roles of virtual characters and, through these characters, interact with the game world and others. World of Warcraft, EverQuest and Ultima Online are a few popular examples.

MSN – (Microsoft Network)

This is the full range of internet services provided by Microsoft, but its dominant use is reserved for MSN Messenger, a software program for real time conversation with one or more contacts, using text, voice and video stream.

Multitasking
Deceptive naming of a process that is actually better described as queued or fast switching serial task completion. A user may store several tasks in active memory while keeping track of possible relevant inputs to process and deciding to raise necessary attention for processing information or task completion.

Networks: human and technical
Networks are a web of nodes and connections. In technical (computer) networks, nodes are typically the computers themselves and the connections made between them are wires and cables transmitting electrical signals, often through switch points. Human networks consist of people and the relations they maintain. For someone to maintain relations, a measure of trust is required. Some connections may be used more often than others and it's frequently seen that the web of a network is a living organism with nodes adding and leaving and connections being broken and (re)formed.

Online game
A form of computer game, where the gamer has to connect his or her computer to the internet. There are online games against artificial intelligence, requiring nothing more than a web browser, but there are also many online games where the user connects to a community of players for multiplayer gaming, either in teams or against each other. Some multiplayer online games require that you first buy and install the game on your local computer, before connecting.

P2P- (Peer to peer networking)
P2P networks use distributed means of traffic management and computing. This contrasts with the common usage for information resources that are stored in centralized servers. In P2P networks there is no central hierarchy and every node in the network is simultaneously receiving and supplying information. The most popular use made of P2P today is the sharing of audio, video and data files. Software that makes use of P2P for file sharing purposes include LimeWire, eMule, KaZaa, and Tribler.

Podcast

The name for both the delivery mechanism and content of multimedia streams. The term is derived from the use of the popular iPod media player and the type of delivery (broadcasting). Much like radio, you have to tune into or subscribe to a stream. Formats used to deliver podcasts are Atom or RSS.

Real Time Strategy (RTS) (games)

Strategic (warfare) game, modelled on table top games like Risk or, more recently, Settlers of Catan. In a top down view, players usually represent the generals and decision makers. Players will be motivated to gather resources or troops to attain or conquer goals.

RPG – (Role-Playing Game)

The term can be used for any type of game or play where the players simulate roles or aspects of themselves. A role-playing game typically involves a 'game world' with set rules and characteristics (much like physics in our 'real' world), where players are then free to improvise within the limits of their role. During game play, the players will usually collaboratively add some history/story to the game world or follow a set storyline to completion. RPG is a very popular genre both in table top and computer gaming. Popular examples include the Dungeons & Dragons series as well as the traditional children's game, cowboys and Indians.

RSS feed

Abbreviation for both 'Rich Site Summary' and 'Really Simple Syndication': an RSS feed is a digest of important information being tracked. For instance, one can have a RSS feed from a news site like CNN.com, relaying the latest updates. Feeds can contain both multimedia information as links to such resources and typically require a piece of software to interpret and display them.

Shoot 'em up (games)

Version of warfare gaming where players typically use a variety of weapons to inflict maximum damage or multiple deaths (also referred to as frags or kills). Game types may include single play against artificial intelligence, team play or player versus player and may include goals such as 'capture the flag'. Non-computer game forms include paintball and laser gaming.

Skype (*see also* VoIP)
Software for connecting one's computer with other computers or telephones, supporting voice, video and text conversation.

Smileys
A means of using punctuation to display emotional states and thus increase the information capacity of text only communication; also referred to as emoticons.

Examples include :-) for a happy face, :-P or :P for a joking face (tongue sticking out of the corner of its mouth) or :(for a sad face; the colon usually denotes the eyes. Typically tilt your head to the left to interpret a smiley. In modern software, combinations forming smileys are often replaced by icons.

Social software
Any software tool that facilitates people to communicate and collaborate online, forming communities, and giving control to the end users to manipulate content and functionalities. Social software focus on community building through identity and virtual presence. Social software is a family of applications that conforms to the Web 2.0 philosophy. Examples include Flickr, Del.icio.us and Wikipedia.

VoIP – (Voice-over IP)
Traditional telephone systems work by setting up continuous streams between point A and B for each conversation. As bandwidth is reserved for the entire duration of the conversation, not speaking is relatively costly. An alternative was found in providing speech through standard Internet Protocol (IP), where speech is sent as individual packets that use no more bandwidth than required for transmission. VoIP is also used as a term for software allowing a computer user to directly speak with others

through their internet connection. Skype is a popular application for VoIP, also allowing IP-to-phone translation, but many other applications including, for instance, MSN, contain similar basic audio functions.

Wiki
A wiki is a collaborative writing tool for the web. It allows any user to quickly add or edit content. For example, www.wikipedia.org is a large free online encyclopedia, constantly updated by anyone who feels the need to do so.

WinRAR
A program that uses compression algorithms on files to reduce their size in bytes, without loss of information (*see also* Compression algorithm)

Zapping
The process of switching from and to different information streams, as is done, for instance, with a television set and remote control device when changing channels. Typically, zapping is a method for increasing the density of interesting information in time; a form of efficient time management.

Bibliography

Aarseth, E. (2001), 'Computer Game Studies, Year One', *Games Studies 1/1* (July), www.gamestudies.org/0101/editorial.html, 16-06-2004

Barham, N. (2004), *Disconnected: Why Your Kids Are Turning Their Backs on Everything We Thought We Knew*, Ebury Press, London

Barone, C. (2005), 'The New Academy', *Educating the Net-generation*, www.educause.edu/TheNewAcademy/6068, 13-07-05

Brown, M. (2005) 'Learning Spaces', *Educating the Net-generation*, www.educause.edu/LearningSpaces/6072, 13-07-05

Castells, M. (2003), *The Internet Galaxy: Reflections on the Internet, Business, and Society*, Oxford University Press, Oxford

Dallow, P. (2001), 'The Space of Information: Digital Media as Simulation of the Analogical Mind'. In Munt, S. (ed), *Technospaces: Inside the New Media*, Continuum, London, New York, pp.57–70

Daniel, J. (1996), *Mega-Universities and Knowledge Media: Technology Strategies for Higher Education*, Kogan Page, London

Davies, C., Hayward, G. & Lukman, L. (2005), '14–19 and Digital Technologies: A review of research and projects', *NESTA Futurelab*, Bristol, www.nestafuturelab.org/research/reviews/reviews_13/13_01 .htm, 01-06-05

Dede, C. (2005), 'Planning for Neomillennial Learning Styles: Implications for Investments in Technology and Faculty', *Educating the Net-generation*, www.educause.edu/ir/library/pdf/eqm0511.pdf, 07-11-05

Eskelinen, M. (2001), 'The Gaming Situation', *Games Studies 1/1* (July), www.gamestudies.org/0101/eskelinen/, 01-07-04

Fagerjord, A. (2003), 'Rhetorical Convergence: Studying Web Media'. In Morrison, G., Liestøl, A. & Rasmussen, T. (eds), *Digital Media Revisited; Theoretical and Conceptual Innovation in Digital Domains*, MIT Press, Cambridge, Mass. London

Fogg, B.J. (2003), *Persuasive Technology: Using Computers to Change What We Think and Do*, Morgan Kaufmann, San Francisco, Calif.

Gee, J.P. (2003), *What Video Games Have to Teach Us About Learning and Literacy*, Palgrave Macmillan, New York

Gonzalez, C. (2004), 'The Role of Blended Learning in the World of Technology', www.unt.edu/benchmarks/archives/2004/september04/eis. htm, 11-09-05

Goodson, I, Knobel, M., Lankshear, C. & Mangan, M. (2002), *Cyber Spaces/Social Spaces: Culture Clash in Computerized Classrooms*, Palgrave Macmillan, New York

Hartman, J, Moskal, P. & Dziuban, C. (2005), 'Preparing the Academy of Today for the Learner of Tomorrow', *Educating the Net-generation*, www.educause.edu/PreparingtheAcademyofTodayforthe LearnerofTomorrow/6062, 13-07-05

Herz, J.C. (2001), 'Gaming the system: what higher education can learn from multiplayer online worlds', www.educause.edu/ir/library/pdf/ffpiu019.pdf, 05-08-03

Hird, A. (2000), *Learning from Cyber-Savvy Students: How Internet-Age Kids Impact Classroom Teaching*, Stylus, Sterling, Va

Huitt, W. (2001), 'Motivation to learn: An overview', *Educational Psychology Interactive*, Valdosta State University, Valdosta, Ga http://chiron.valdosta.edu/whuitt/col/motivation/motivate. html, 20-02-06

Huysmans, F., Haan de, J. & Broek van den, A. (2004), 'Achter de schermen: Een kwart eeuw lezen, luisteren, kijken en internetten', www.scp.nl/publicaties/boeken/9037701299/AchterDeScher men.pdf, 25-11-04

Jacobs, F. (2002), 'Interactie met ICT in het leerproces: noodzaak tot dialoog onomstotelijk aanwezig', *Informatie*, November 2002, www.edusite.nl/edusite/publicaties/11514

Kirriemuir, J. & McFarlane, A. (2004), 'Literature Review in Games and Learning', *Report 8, NESTA Futurelab*, Bristol, www.nestafuturelab.org/research/reviews/08_01.htm, 08-06-05

Kolb, D.A. (1984), *Experiential Learning*, Prentice Hall, Englewood Cliffs, NJ

Kurzweil, R. (1999), *The Age of Spiritual Machines: When Computers Exceed Human Intelligence*, Viking Penguin, New York

Kvavik, R. (2005), 'Convenience, Communications, and Control: How Students Use Technology', *Educating the Net-generation,*
www.educause.edu/ConvenienceCommunicationsand
Control%3AHowStudentsUseTechnology/6070, 13-07-05

Lanestedt (2003), 'The Challenge of Digital Learning Environments in Higher Education: The Need for a Merging of Perspectives on Standardization'. In Morrison, G., Liestøl, A. & Rasmussen, T. (eds), *Digital Media Revisited; Theoretical and Conceptual Innovation in Digital Domains*, MIT Press, Cambridge, Mass. London

Lankshear, C. & Knobel, M. (2003), *New Literacies: Changing knowledge in the classroom*, Open University Press, Buckingham

Lindström, M. & Seybold, P. (2003), *Brandchild: remarkable insights into the minds of today's global kids and their relationships with brands*, Kogan Page, London

Lippincott, J. (2005), 'Net-generation Students and Libraries', *Educating the Net-generation*,
www.educause.edu/NetGenerationStudentsandLibraries/
6067, 13-07-05

Maslow, A.H. (1987), *Motivation and Personality*, 3rd edn, Addison-Wesley, New York

Mayer, I. & Veeneman, W. (eds), (2002), *Games in a World of Infrastructures: Simulation-games for Research, Learning and Intervention*, Eburon, Delft

McMahan, A. (2003), 'Immersion, Engagement, and Presence: a Method for Analysing 3-D Video Games'. In Wolf, M.J.P. & Perron, B. (eds), 2003, *The Video Game Theory Reader*, Routledge, New York

Milton, J. (2004), 'Literature Review in Languages, Technologies and Learning', *NESTA Futurelab*, Bristol,
www.nestafuturelab.org/research/reviews/lang01.htm,
07-07-05

Moore, A., Moore, J, & Fowler, S. (2005), 'Faculty Development for the Net-generation', Educating the Net-generation, www.educause.edu/FacultyDevelopmentfortheNet Generation/6071, 13-07-05

Naismith, L., Lonsdale, P., Vavoula, G. & Sharples, M. (2005), 'Literature Review in Mobile Technologies and Learning', Report 11, NESTA Futurelab, Bristol, www.nestafuturelab.org/research/reviews/reviews_11_and 12/11_01.htm, 07-05-05

NEA (2006), 'The Future of Higher Education', www.nea.org/he/future/index.html, 30-05-2006

Negroponte, N. (1995), *Being Digital*, Vintage, Vancouver

Oblinger, D. (2004), 'The Next Generation of Educational Engagement', *Journal of Interactive Media in Education*, 2004 (8). Special Issue on the Educational Semantic Web, www.jime.open.ac.uk/2004/8, 08-09-05

Oblinger, D., Martin R. & Baer, L. (2004), 'Unlocking the potential of gaming technology', National Learning Infrastructure Initiative Annual Meeting, 26 January 2004, San Diego, Calif.

Oblinger, D. & Oblinger, J. (eds), (2005), *Educating the Netgeneration*, Educause, USA www.educause.edu/educatingthenetgen, 13-07-05

OECD (2004), Schooling for tomorrow: The role of ICT in the OECD/Ceri Schooling Scenarios, www.oecd.org/dataoecd/41/62/32503182.pdf

O'Reily, T. (2005), 'What Is Web 2.0, Design Patterns and Business Models for the Next Generation of Software', www.oreillynet.com/pub/a/oreilly/tim/news/2005/09/30/ what-is-web-20.html

Papert, S. (1998), 'Does Easy Do It? Children, Games, and Learning'. In *Game Developer Magazine*, p.88, www.papert.org/articles/Doeseasydoit.html

Prensky, M. (2001), *Digital Game-Based Learning*, McGraw-Hill, New York

Prensky, M. (2002), 'What Kids Learn That's POSITIVE From Playing Video Games', www.marcprensky.com/writing/Prensky%20%20What%20 Kids%20Learn%20Thats%20POSITIVE%20From%20Playing %20Video%20Games.pdf, 20-06-04

Roberts, G. (2005), 'Technology and Learning Expectations of the Net-generation', *Educating the Net-generation*, www.educause.edu/TechnologyandLearningExpectationsof theNetGeneration/6056, 13-07-05

Rosser, J. (2004), 'Video Gamers Make Good Surgeons', www.cbsnews.com/stories/2004/04/07/health/main610601. shtml

Seely Brown, J. (2001), 'The Social Life of Information: Learning in the Digital Age', *Educause* www.educause.edu/asp/doclib/abstract.asp?ID=EDU0145, 21-10-01

Siemens, G. (2004), 'Connectivism: A Learning Theory for the Digital Age', www.elearnspace.org/Articles/connectivism.htm, 01-06-06

Sousa, D. (2001), *How the Brain Learns: A Classroom Teacher's Guide*, Corwin Press Inc., Thousands Oaks, Calif.

Squire, K.D. & Steinkuhler, C.A. (2005), 'Meet the Gamers: Games as Sites for New Information Literacies', *Library Journal*, www.libraryjournal.com/article/CA516033.html, 01-07-2005

Staalduinen, J.P. van (2004), 'Toekomstverkenning Onderwijs Ondersteunende Infrastructuur', *TU Delft internal publication*, Delft

Star, J. (2004), 'The Edinburgh scenarios: Global scenarios for the future of e-Learning', presentation at eLearn International 2004, www.elearninternational.co.uk/2004/test/2004/presentations/sidlaw/thurs/jonothan_star_thurs.zip, 10-05-2006

Tapscott, D. (1998), *Growing up Digital: The Rise of the Net-Generation*, McGraw-Hill, New York

Turkle, S. (1997), *Life on the Screen: Identity in the Age of the Internet*, Simon & Schuster Inc., New York

Veen, W. (2000), 'Flexibel onderwijs voor nieuwe generaties studerenden', *Intreerede* 15-12-2000, http://elearning.surf.nl/docs/e-learning/oratiewimveen2.pdf, 01-08-2003

Veen, W. & Jacobs. F. (2005), *Leren van Jongeren: Een literatuuronderzoek naar nieuwe geletterdheid*, SURF, Utrecht, The Netherlands

Veen, W. & Vrakking, B. (2006), 'Hoe de TU Delft over 5 jaar onderwijs moet aanbieden: Beleidsvoorbereidend onderzoek naar de behoeften en mening van studenten ten aanzien van de inzet van ICT in het onderwijs', TU Delft internal publication, Delft

Zuidweg, M. (2002), 'Nieuw! Anders!', *NRC Handelsblad*, Saturday 5/Sunday 6 October, 2002, Science & Education section, p.39

Acknowledgements

With thanks to the following for permission to reproduce text, screenshots and photographs in this book.

Cuteoverload for screenshot from www.cuteoverload.com

Delft University of Technology for screenshot from www.etrax.tbm.tudelft.nl

Jonathan Star for figures 6.1 & 6.2 (www.elearninternational.co.uk/2004/test/2004/ presentations/sidlaw/thurs/jonothan_star_thurs.zip)

J.P. van Staalduinen for figure 6.3

Linux Journal website for quote from 'Interview: Richard Thieme' by Mick Bauer www.linuxjournal.com/article/7934

Google for screenshot from www.blogger.com

Massachusetts Institute of Technology for screenshot from www.DSpace.org, © MIT 2006

Netvibes for screenshot from www.netvibes.com

Skype for screenshot from www.skype.com

Scholierenlab for screenshot from www.scholierenlab.tudelft.nl

Wisdom Quotes for quotes on pages 7, 15, 79, 99 and 111, ©1995–2006 Jone Johnson Lewis, www.wisdomquotes.com

Wikipedia for screenshot from www.wikipedia.org

World of Warcraft for screenshot from www.wow-europe.com

Yahoo! Inc. for screenshots from www.flickr.com and http://del.icio.us

Index

attention levels   28, 33, 61, 62, 63

behaviourism   104, 108
blogs   44, 57–8, 91, 141
books   28, 30, 92

challenge   40, 48, 75, 84, 87, 124
change   16–25, 50–1
   adapting to change   24, 91–3, 95–7, 99–100, 111
   in schools   13–14, 126–32
   technological change   28, 107–8, 109
cheating   48, 59–60, 141–2
cognitivism   104
collaboration   11, 41, 48, 49, 73–4, 92–3, 103
communication   92–3, 95–6
   and learning   80–1, 106
   networks   29–30, 42, 48, 49, 58, 101
   technology   19–20, 29–30, 31–2, 38–9, 49, 90, 101
competition   73, 88
computer games
   challenge   40, 48, 84, 87
   as community activity   40–1, 54–5, 73–4
   and gender   38–9
   and learning   11, 48, 51, 75

non-linear behaviour   32–3
play   28, 30, 38, 39–40, 84, 87, 90–1
computers   30, 46
confidence   48
connectivism   105
constructivism   11, 96, 104–6, 107
control   37, 40, 42, 63, 75, 96, 137
copying   80, 108, 109, 122
copyright   47, 142
creativity   18, 22, 23, 25, 75, 96, 109–10
curricula   13, 50, 129

Del.icio.us   76–7
discovery   48, 92, 103
diversity   129
DSpace   51–2

Edinburgh scenarios   112–15, 119, 120
education
   changes in schools   13–14, 126–32
   current challenges   100–10
   design principles   121–6
   future scenarios   112–21
   learning theories   11, 96, 103–7
   new initiatives   12–14, 132–9

technological change   107–8, 109

E-merge scenarios   115–17, 120

entrepreneurship   23–4, 106

E-Trax   93–5

exams   128–9

experience   21

experimentation   48, 109, 121

feedback   48, 108–9

flexibility   13, 23, 126–7

Flickr.com   44, 47

'43 Things'   45

gender issues   38–9

globalization   19, 29

glossary   141–8

goods   17, 21

homework   33–4, 59, 60, 130

Homo zappiens   10–11, 12, 27–34, 36–45, 48–51, 102, 143–4

iconic skills   55–6, 58–60

images   30, 43–4, 66, 67–8, 72, 95, 136–8

imagination   91

immersion   40, 48, 75, 124–5

individualization   95, 106

industry   18, 21

information
  acquisition   81
  concepts   67
  detail   67
  filtering   30, 37, 59, 63, 72
  keywords   69, 72
  overload/richness   59, 67, 69
  processing   11, 62, 63, 66–8, 69
  reference memory   76–7
  retrieval   58–9, 60, 69, 76–7
  sources   30, 36, 69
  transparency   21
  trustworthiness   59–60, 71

internet   34–5, 37, 43–8, 55–60, 70–1, 101–2, 107

knowledge   11, 22, 109

LAN (Local Area Network) parties 40–1, 54–5

leadership   73

learning
  adapting to change   24, 91–3, 95–7, 99–100, 111
  communication   80–1, 106
  and computer games   11, 48, 51, 75
  e-Learning   143
  goals   69, 72, 109
  influence of technology   49, 90–1, 105, 109
  lifelong learning   121
  non-linear approach   32–3, 68–9, 72, 75, 106
  potential   109
  reasons for learning   80–1
  skills   13, 49, 51, 81
  and technology skills   51, 53, 55–6, 58–63, 65–9, 72–5

learning styles   83–4, 87–8, 105–6, 123, 127

learning theories   11, 96, 103–7

mobile phones   30, 42, 50

money   21, 22

motivation   28, 48, 75, 88, 125
  self-motivation   40, 100, 106

MSN   31–2, 61, 67, 145

multitasking   33, 60–3, 65, 144

NEA scenarios   119

Netvibes   70–1

networks   13, 29–30, 42, 48, 49, 58, 71, 101, 145

non-linear behaviour   32–3, 68–9, 72, 75, 106

OECD scenarios   117, 118

organization skills   73

parental concerns   28, 50–1

passion   125

passivity   50

PDP (Personal Development Plans)   23–4

physical exercise   81, 89–90

planning   73

play   81–4
    computer games   28, 30, 38,
        39–40, 84, 87, 90–1
    and learning   11, 75, 103, 109
    playground games   42
poverty   46
privacy   44–5
problem solving   11, 13, 48–9,
    73, 74, 75, 126

reading skills   56, 67, 68–9
relevance   122–3
responsibility   125–6
risk-taking   23

scanning   56, 67, 69
school   34, 49–50
    see also education
self-direction   125
self-esteem   48
self-expression   96, 100
self-knowledge   96
services   22, 71
simulation   84, 89, 90–1
skimming   58
Skype   85–6, 147
/21 (Slash21)   132–8
SMS language   49, 67, 68
SMS messages   36, 50
social constructivism   104–5
social context   28
social interaction   81–3, 89–90
social skills   28, 73–4
social software   44, 147
specialization   18, 95, 104, 131
StudentLab   64–5
subjects   131, 135

talent   123, 127
teachers   12–13, 107, 125–6,
    133–5
teaching   21, 28, 80
technology
    and change   28, 107–8, 109
    communication   19–20,
        29–30, 31–2, 38–9, 49, 90,
        101
    expertise   32–3, 36–7
    future scenarios   112–15
    influence on learning   49,
        90–1, 105, 109
    skills   51, 53, 55–6, 58–63,
        65–9, 72–5
television   30, 63, 65
    see also zapping
texts   55–6, 68–9
themes   135, 137–8
time slots   24, 130–1
trust   59–60, 71, 122
tutors   133–5

values   22, 25, 81
virtual communities   40, 42, 45,
    74
VoIP (Voice-over IP)   74, 85–6,
    147–8

weblogs see blogs
Wikipedia   34–5, 46, 71
wikis   34, 91, 148
World of Warcraft   40, 42–3,
    73–4
www.homozappiens.nl   8–9

year programmes   127–8

zapping   33, 55, 63, 65–8, 148

Homo Zappiens: Growing up in a digital age